MOSIN-NAGANT MODEL 1891

Facts and Circumstance in the History and Development of the Mosin-Nagant Family of Rifles

by

Frederic Faust

Mosin Nagant M1891:
Facts and Circumstance in the History and Development of the Mosin-Nagant Family of Rifles

by Frederic Faust

© Copyright 2021 - All rights reserved.

ISBN: 978-0-934523-49-3

Editor@Middle-Coast-Publishing.com

Good Books Are Where We Find Our Dreams

Table of Contents

Dedication 1

The Oath of the Red Army (1918) 2

The Oath of War 1939 3

Meet the Inventors 5

Major General Sergio Ivanovich Mosin 5

Léon Henri Nagant de Deuxchaisnes 6

The Nagant M1895 Revolver 7

Sites Where Mosin-Nagant Rifles and Carbines Were Built 8

    The Tula Arms Plant 8

    The Izhevsk Arsenal 9

    The Sestroretsk Arms Factory 9

Mosin-Nagant Specifications 10

Genesis of the Mosin-Nagant 13

The Siege of Plevna 13

A Call for Designs 14

The German Mauser 1898 Versus 1891 Mosin 15

Refinement and Production 18

Nagant's Legal Dispute 18

The Russo-Japanese War 1904 – 1905 20

World War I 21

Civil War – 1917 Russian Revolution 22

The Winter War 1939-1940 22

The Great Patriotic War/World War II 25

- Increased Worldwide Use 27
- Mosin-Nagant Variants 28
  - Mosin-Nagant Model 1891 Infantry Rifle 29
  - Mosin-Nagant Model 1891 Dragoon Rifle 30
  - The Cossack Rifle 30
  - Mosin-Nagant Model 1907 Carbine 32
  - Mosin-Nagant Model 1891/30 32
  - Mosin-Nagant Model 1938 Carbine 33
  - Mosin-Nagant M44 Carbine 33
  - Mosin-Nagant M59 Carbine 34
  - The 91/30 Sniper Rifle 34
  - Mosin-Nagant 1891 Obrez 38
  - Ots-48/OTs-48K (short) Sniper Rifles 38
  - The Republic of Estonia 39
  - The Republic of Finland 41
  - M/91 Ulaani Carbine 44
  - M/24 - The Lotta Rifle 45
  - M/28 46
  - M/28-30 47
  - Finnish M39 47
  - Finland's Simo Häyhä 50
- Czechoslovakia 51
- The People's Republic of China 51
  - Chinese Type 53 Carbine 51
- Hungary 52

Section	Page
Romania	53
Poland	54
Polish Variants	55
The United States of America	56
U.S. Rifle, 7.62 mm Model of 1916	56
New England Westinghouse Built Mosin-Nagants	56
Remington-Built Mosin-Nagant's	57
U.S. Rifle, 7.62 mm Model of 1916 In Military Hands	59
Re-Purposed Mosin M1916s	62
Civilian Use	64
40.8-mm Dyakanov Rifle Grenade Launcher	67
Mosin-Nagant Accessories	69
Field Stripping the Mosin-Nagant	71
How to Disassemble the Magazine Floorplate	73
The 7.62 X 54R Cartridge	74
The Lineage of the 7.62 X 54mm R Cartridge	75
7.62×53mmR (Finland) Versus 7.62×54mmR (Russia)	76
Deciphering a Spam Can	77
Basic Specifications 21st-Century Russian Military Loads	78
Cartridge Designations	79
Identifying Crates, Tins, and Wrapping	81
A Word About ShKAS Ammo	82
The Fighting Weapons of Seven Warring Powers	86
Glossary	89

Dedication

This comprehensive compilation of Mosin-Nagant knowledge is dedicated to the Soviet soldiers, affectionately known as *frontovik,* who valiantly fought in the Great Patriotic War, brave men and women whose courage and dedication defeated the Nazi war machine. And of course it is further dedicated to the soldiers of the Czar Nicholas II who fought the Imperial German war machine.

The Soviet Rifleman

The Soviet rifleman known as a *peshkom* (on foot), or as a *frontovik.* - Every year, Soviet men received draft notices in the mail informing them to report for duty at a collection point with a bag carrying spare clothes, underwear, and tobacco.

Conscripts boarded a train bound for a reception center where they were issued uniforms, underwent a physical, had their heads shaven, and were given a steam bath to rid them of lice. The soldier was issued ammo pouches, shelter-cape, ration bag, cooking pot, water bottle, and an identity tube containing papers listing pertinent personal information.

During training, conscripts were awakened between 5 and 6 am. The training lasted for 10 to 12 hours six days out of the week. After finishing training, enlistees and conscripts solemnly took the Oath of the Red Army.

The Oath of the Red Army (1918)

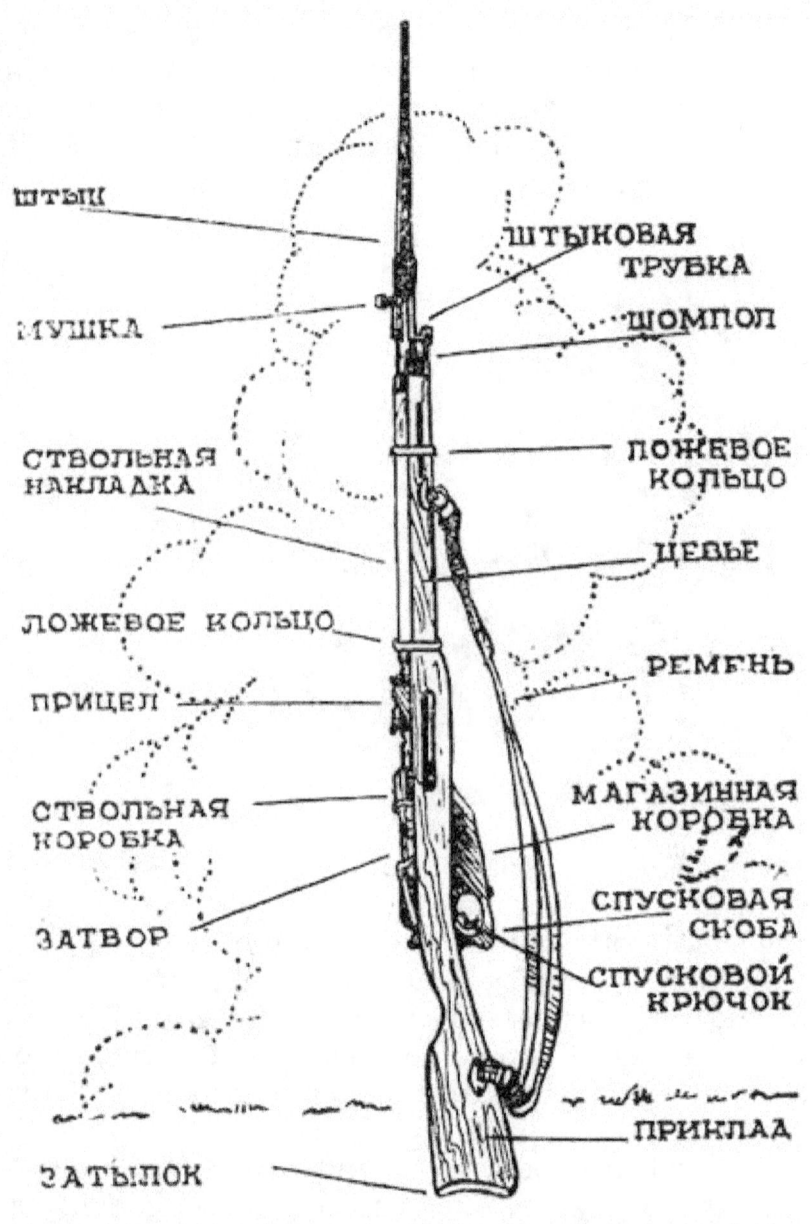

I, Ivan Petrovich, a citizen of the Union of the Soviet Socialist Republics, entering into the ranks of the Red Army of the Workers and Peasants', take this oath and solemnly promise to be an honest, brave, disciplined, vigilant fighter, staunchly to protect military and state secrets, and unquestioningly to obey all military regulations and orders of commanders and superiors.

I promise conscientiously to study military affairs, in every way to protect state secrets and state property, and to my last breath to be faithful to the people, the Soviet Motherland, and the Workers-Peasants' Government. I am always prepared on order of the Workers and Peasants Government to rise to the defense of my Motherland, the Union of Soviet Socialist Republics; and as a fighting man of the Red Army of Workers and Peasants', I promise to defend it bravely, skillfully, with dignity and honor, sparing neither my blood nor my life itself for the achievement of total victory over our enemies.

If by evil intent I should violate this, my solemn oath, then let the severe punishment of Soviet law and the total hatred and contempt of the working classes befall me.

The Oath of War 1939

By Markov Borisovich Grinberg (1907-2003)

Taken a scant few moments before his regiment attacked an entrenched German defensive position, the above photo shows a Soviet soldier kissing his gun.. During World War II, Markov-Grinberg served first as a soldier and later in the war as a war correspondent for Slovo Boitsa, a military publication. (Word of Soldier)

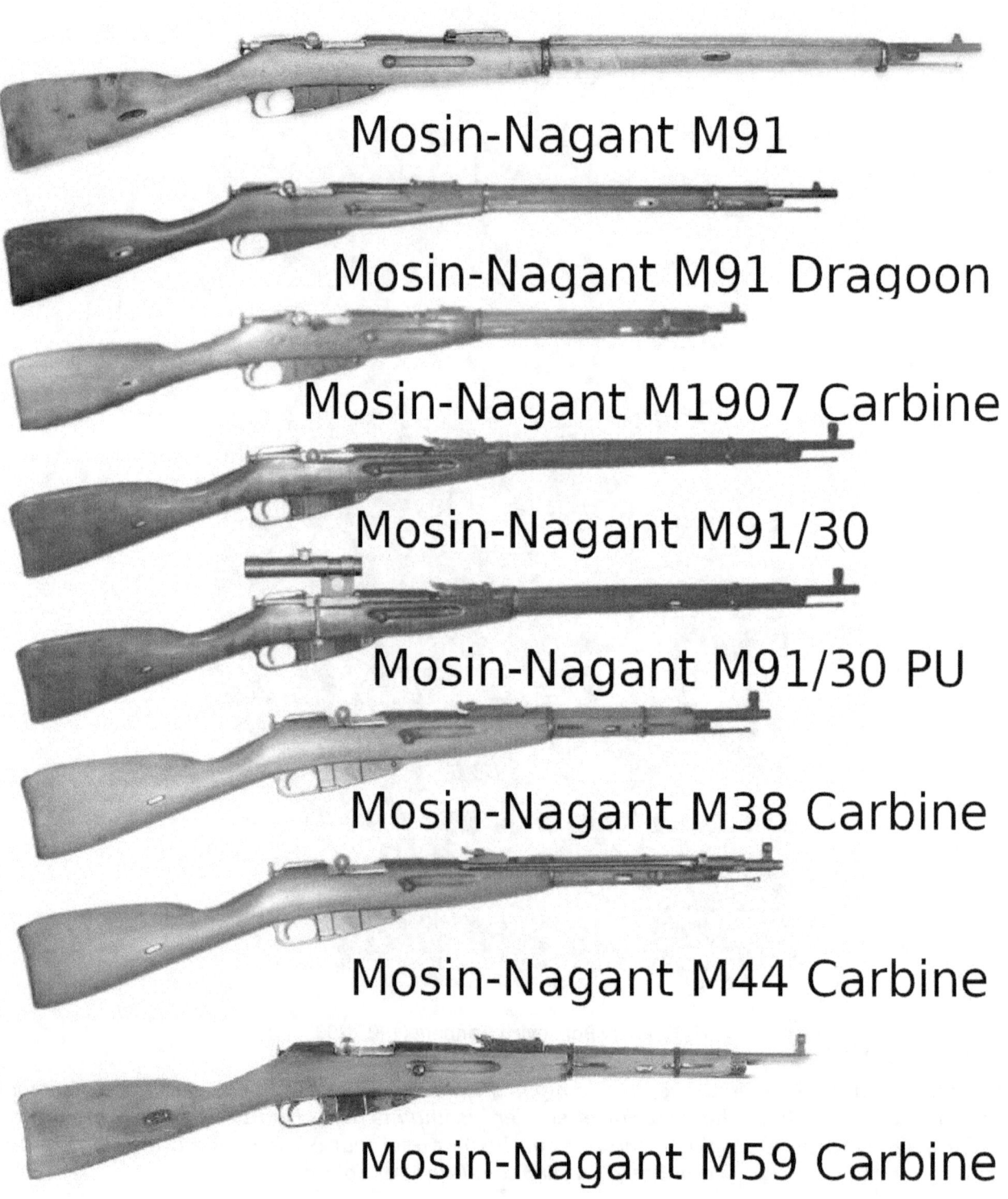

Meet the Inventors

Major General Sergio Ivanovich Mosin

Major General Sergio Ivanovich Mosin (Cyrillic: Серге́й Ива́нович Мо́син) was an Imperial Russian army officer and designer associated with the Tula Arms Plant. Born in 1849, Mosin, the son of a retired Second Lieutenant, entered the Mikhailovsky Artillery School in 1872, graduated in 1875, and took employment at the Tula Arms Plant. Working his way up the ranks at the Tula Arms Plant, Mosin became acting chairman of the plant's admission division. He oversaw the production of rifles at the Sestroretsk and Izhevsk Arms Factories.

Mosin participated in devising Damascus steel technology used in the production of barrels. In 1889, Mosin met Belgian gunsmith Léon Nagant. The two collaborated on the design of the Mosin Nagant rifle. Mosin died February 8, 1902, in Sestroretsk at the age of 52, of pneumonia.

Léon Henri Nagant de Deuxchaisnes

Born in Liège in 1833, Léon Nagant was a Belgian automobile and firearms designer. Nagant and Colonel Sergei Ivanovitch Mosin most famously designed one of the oldest military rifles still in service, the venerable Mosin-Nagant M1891.

Similarly, one of the oldest revolvers remaining in service is the Russian M1895 Nagant, a seven-shot, gas-seal revolver designed by Léon and his brother, Émile Nagant. Russian army troops used to praise the weapon's robust nature, saying if anything went wrong with it, it was possible to fix it with a few blows from a hammer. The Nagant brothers also figured prominently in the design and manufacture of the Remington rolling block rifle.

The Nagant M1895 Revolver

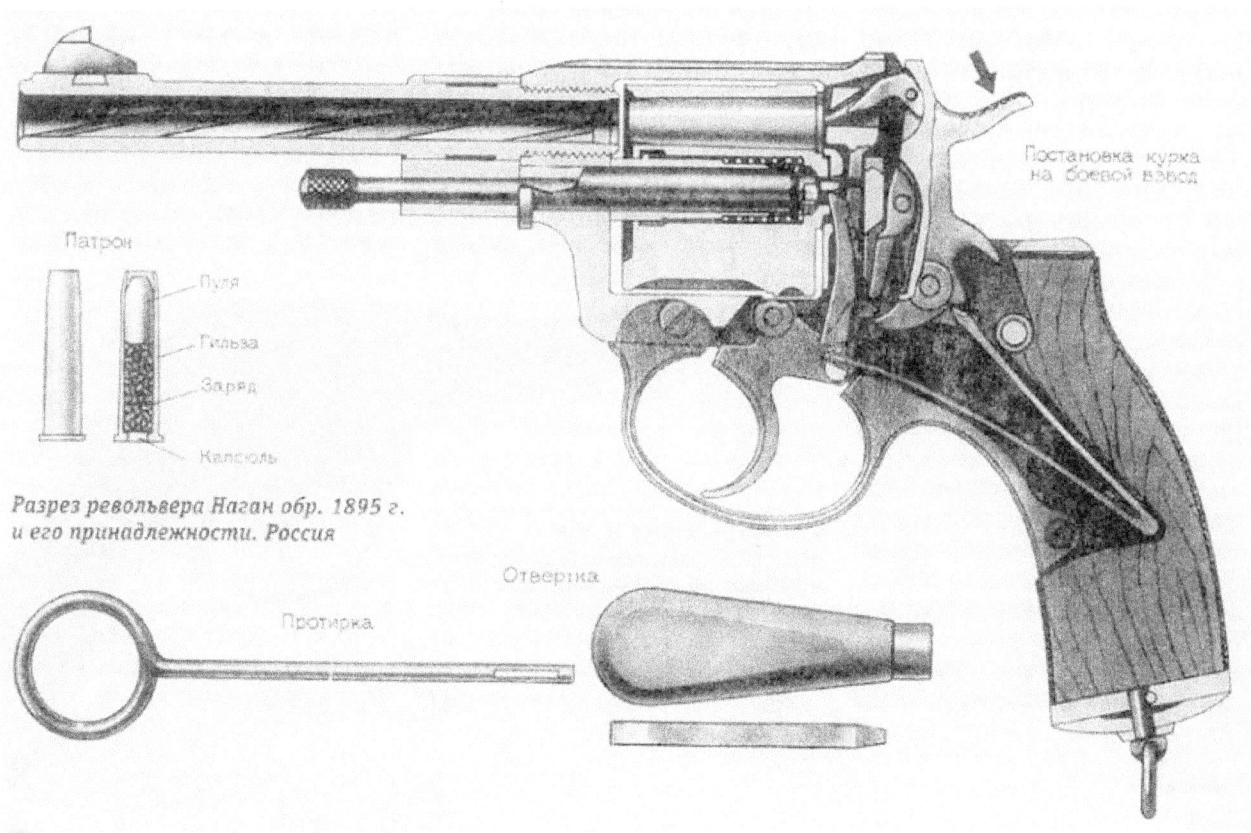

Sights	Fixed front post and rear notch
Caliber	7.62 38mmR
Barrel length	10.5 inches/ 235 mm
Muzzle Velocity	891 fps/272 ms
Weight	1.8 Pounds/ .9 Kg
Cylinder	7-rounds
Action	Double action/Single action
Effective range	150 yard/ 46 m
Rate of fire	14-21 rounds per minute

Sites Where Mosin-Nagant Rifles and Carbines Were Built

The family of Mosin Nagants was built in Russian and the United States of America. In Russia, the firearms factories were Tula, Izhevsk, and Sestroretsk. In the United States, at Remington and New England Westinghouse.

The Tula Arms Plant

In 1712, Tsar Peter the Great created the Tula arms plant to arm its citizens against nomadic invasions. Following its 19th century reconstruction, Tula Arms Factory, one of the most prominent arms factories in Europe, began production of the famous Berdan rifle with an improved bolt in 1879.

During the Great Patriotic War, German troops invaded the USSR. By December 5, 1941, the 2nd Panzer Division had advanced to within a few kilometers of the city of Tula. The Soviets rather wisely evacuated Tula Arms Plant.

The Izhevsk Arsenal

A major firearms manufacturer founded in 1942 for manufacturing small arms, one of the primary factories producing Mosin–Nagant and SVT-40 rifles during World War II for issue to Soviet troops. During World War One, more than 1.5 million rifles were manufactured, and during the Great Patriotic War, 11 million rifles and carbines.

The Sestroretsk Arms Factory

Sestroretsk Firearms Factory opened on 27 January 1724. Over time, it grew to become one of the Russian State's biggest and most technically-equipped enterprises, specializing in the manufacture of muskets, rifles, cannons, sabers, rapiers, and cutlasses. It was one of the main arsenals for the production of weapons. Major general Sergei Mosin was the head of the factory from 1894 to 1902. Sestroretsk is located 34 kilometers northwest of St. Petersburg on the shores of the Gulf of Finland, the Sestra River, and the Razliv Lake.

Mosin-Nagant Specifications

Bolt-action rifle	Bolt-action rifle
Place of origin	Russian Empire
Designed	1891
Designers	Captain Sergei Mosin and Léon Nagant
Manufacturers	Tula Izhevsk Sestroryetsk Manufacture Nationale d'Armes de Châtellerault Remington New England Westinghouse
Produced	1891-1965
Number built	37,000,000 (Russia/Soviet Union)
Weight	**M91/30** 4 kg - 8.8 lb **M38** 3.4 kg - 7.5 lb **M44** 4.1 kg - 9.0 lb
Length Overall	**M91/30** 1,232 mm - 48.5 in **Carbines** 1,013 mm - 39.9 in
Barrel length	**M91/30** 730 mm - 29 inches **Carbines** 514 mm - 20.2 inches
Cartridge chambering	7.62×54mmR 7.62×53mmR (Finnish variant) 7.92×57mm Mauser (Polish variants & German captures) 8×50mmR Mannlicher (Austrian captures)

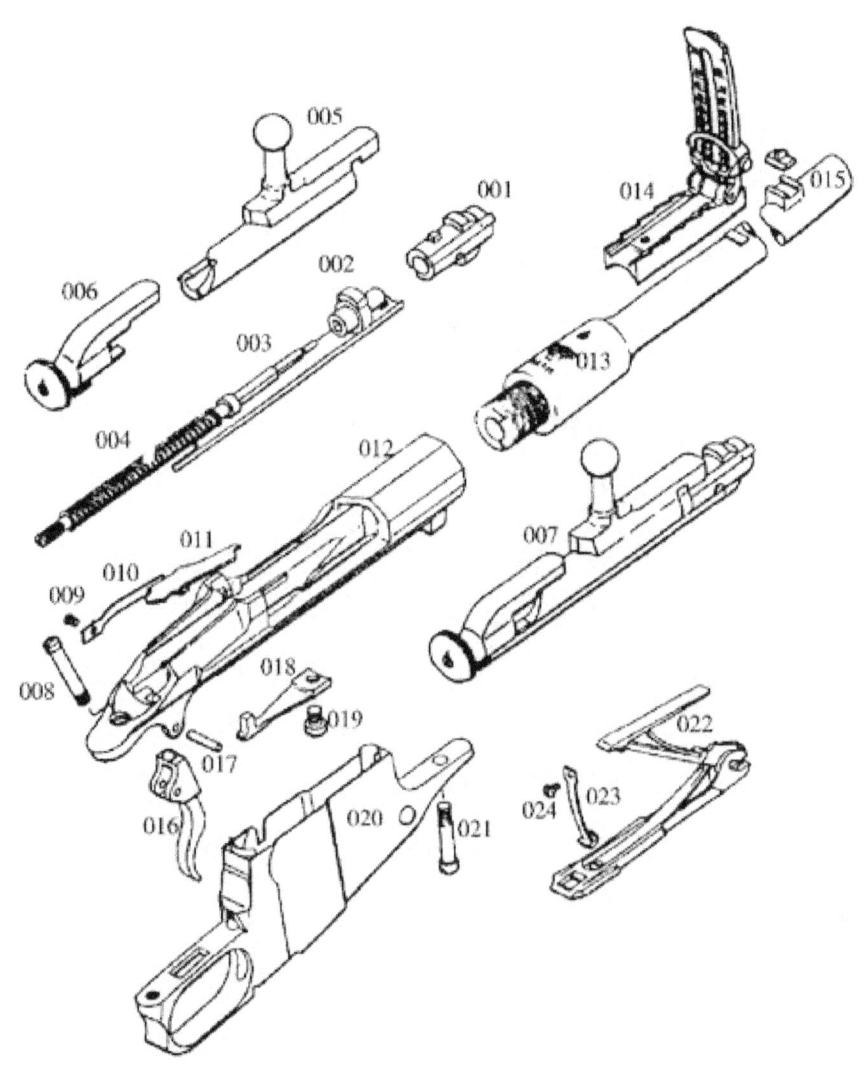

001	bolt head & extractor	013	barrel
002	bolt connector & guide bar	014	rear sight
003	firing pin	015	front sight
004	firing pin spring	016	trigger
005	bolt body	017	trigger hinge pin
006	cocking piece	018	trigger spring & bolt stop
007	bolt assembly	019	bolt stop screw
008	Tang screw	020	trigger guard &magazine
009	ejector spring screw	021	frontguard screw
010	Ejector spring & feed interrupter	022	Magazine spring & floor plate assembly
011	interrupter	023	Floorplate latch
012	receiver	024	Floorplate latch screw .

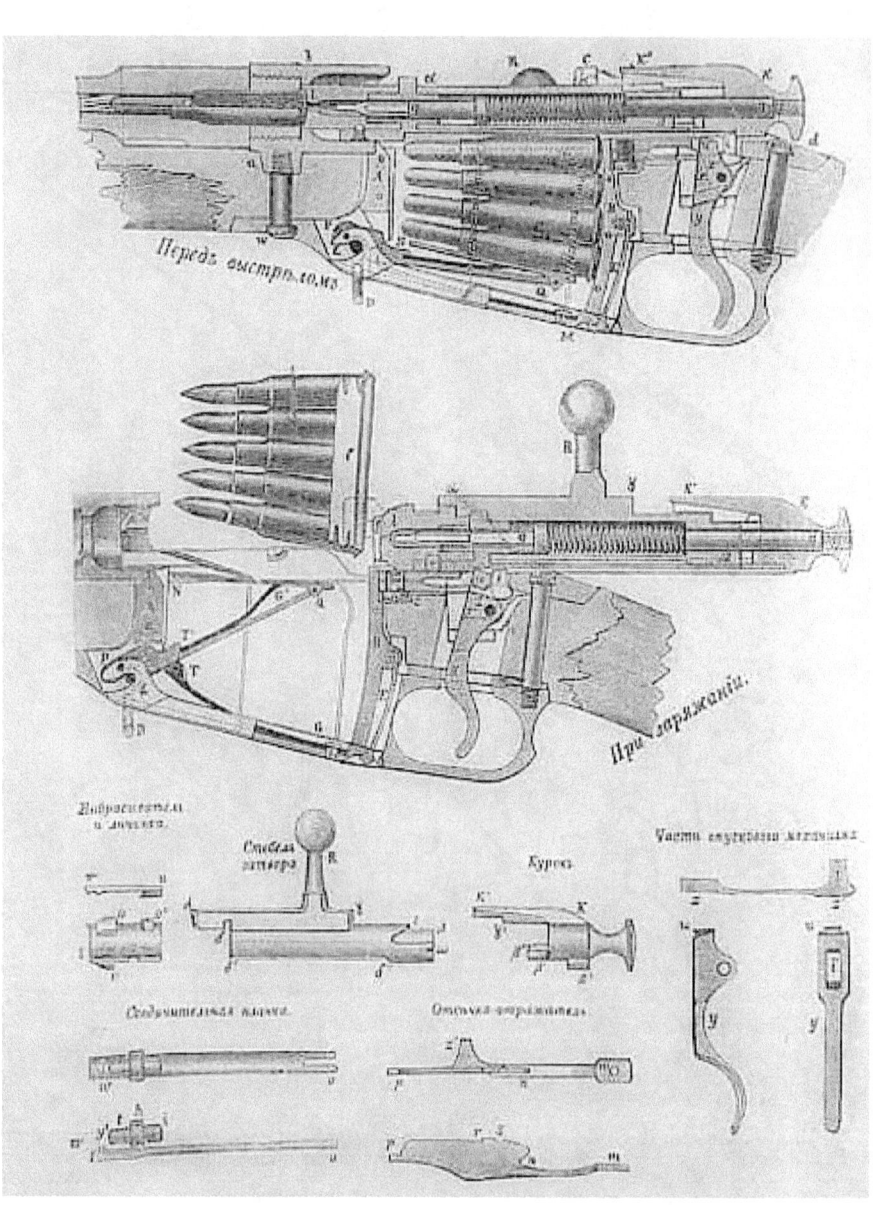

Genesis of the Mosin-Nagant

The Mosin-Nagant (Cyrillic: *Винтовка Мосина*, Vintovka Mosina) is a five-shot, bolt-action, magazine-fed, military rifle, developed by the Imperial Russian Army in 1882-91. Predating the rise of communism, the Russian Empire's armed force put it on active duty. After the Revolution of 1917, it was carried by the Armies of the Soviet Union and various other nations across the globe. It qualifies as *the* most mass-produced military bolt-action rifle in history worldwide. More than 37-million rifles, carbines, and variants ever built.

German and Austrian troops admired the Mosin rifles they captured during the First World War. After World War II, Mosin-Nagants were issued to Soviet Block armies and saw live-fire action in Korea, Vietnam, and Afghanistan.

Long of tooth, Mosin-Nagants continue to turn up in today's Lesser Intensity Conflicts. These bolt guns are plentiful in numbers, reasonably inexpensive to acquire from international arms brokers, boast a rugged character (You can run them over with a truck), are eminently simple to use.

The rifle's lineage began in a hot war back in the 19th century At the bloody Siege of Plevna, during the Russo-Ottoman War of 1877-1878, Russian troops, armed with single-shot rifles, took heavy casualties from Turkish troops armed with Winchester repeating rifles.

The Siege of Plevna

At the siege of Plevna, the Russians and opposing Ottomans carried into battle different styles infantry rifles. Most Russian troops were armed with single-shots, a lifting breech block musket. Adopted by the Russian Empire in 1869, the **M1867 Russian Krnka** (Винтовка Крнка́) was a nothing more than a breech-loading conversion of the muzzle-loading Model 1857. Designed by Czech arms maker Sylvester Krnka, The Tula armory converted the muzzleloaders to breech-loading.

The **Berdan Rifle** (*винтовка Бердана*/*vintovka Berdana* in Russian), created by American firearms expert Hiram Berdan, was standard issue in the Russian Army from 1870 to 1891. While the Berdan rifle replaced the M1867, both it and the Krnka served simultaneously for a time.

Ultimately, after four battles, the Russian forces were victorious at Plevna. That said, it comes as no big surprise to learn Turk's sharpshooting ranks with the more modern single-shot, Peabody Martinique rifle. Even though the Imperial Russian won the battle, the casualties gave the Russian army pause. It was already in the process of equipping troops with the more modern yet still single-shot Berdan rifle. Reports from the front lines of staggeringly heavy losses inflicted upon the Russian Army at Plevna motivated militaries all across Europe to re-equip their armies with repeating rifles, or at the very least to convert existing stores of single-shot rifles into magazine-fed weapons.

At the time of the Plevna Pyrrhic victory, the Russian Army was smack in the middle of re-equipping its troops with the more modern, albeit still single-shot Berdan I (M1868) and Berdan II (M1870) rifles of .42 caliber. But the bloody mauling at Plevna by Turkish sharpshooters repeatedly demonstrated that the Berdan was already obsolescent on introduction.

A Call for Designs

So it came to pass in 1891, two designs competed in Ministry of War trials for a replacement firearm. Namely: The rifles of Captain Sergei Mosin and Belgian engineer Leon Nagant. These entities were radically different from one another. The Russian Mosin was decidedly cruder in its construction, intended to represent the design as a prototype rather than a final design. In contrast, Nagant's rifle was a production model ready for general issue.

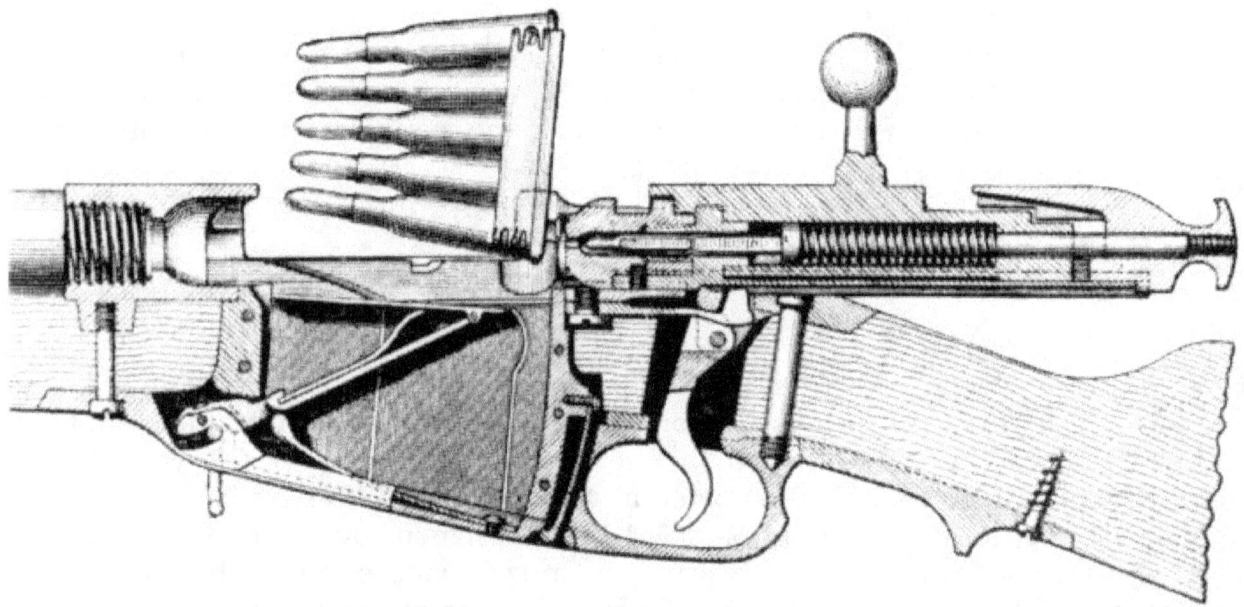

Some firearms aficionados claim the sophistication of the Belgian model worked against it. It was unsuitable for the average, unsophisticated recruit with zero shooting skills. Another strike against it, exorbitant costs. That said, although the three-line looked plain, it quickly showed its robustness, ease of assembly and disassembly, and reliability in adverse conditions. So naturally it followed three rifles were submitted for evaluation:

> Imperial Army Captain Sergei Ivanovich Mosin's **3-line** rifle, chambered 7.62x54r mm.

> Belgian Léon Nagant's a **3.5-line** chambered in .35 caliber (9mm)

Captain Zinoviev also submitted a second 3-line design.

After trials conducted in 1891, evaluators were divided in their assessments. Nagant's rifle was a complicated mechanism. Disassembly was a long and tiresome procedure requiring special tools. Keep in mind, back then, most of the Russian population were unsophisticated peasants.

Mosin's rifles were criticized for their low quality of manufacture and materials, which predictably resulted in stoppages at the firing range. Think Failure To Load, Failure To Fire, Failure To Eject. While the Commission narrowly approved Nagant's rifle with a 14 to 10 vote, General Chagin, head of the Commission, ordered continuing testing. Mosin's rifle showed certain advantages over its competitor, leading to its selection over the Nagant.

Having prevailed over its Not-Invented-Here foreign rival, the 1891 Mosin's first saw the elephant in 1893, in a clash between Russian troops and Afghan tribe members. In 1904
when the Russo-Japanese War began, some three million rifles were in service. Despite a woeful shortage of spare parts and dismal logistical support, the Mosin's design proved its worth in combat conducted in rough terrain and harsh climatic conditions.

The German Mauser 1898 Versus 1891 Mosin

Model 1891 Mosin relied on a pair of (two) front-locking lugs to lock the bolt to the receiver. Mosin lugs lock in a horizontal position, while the German M98 Mauser locks vertically. The Mosin-Nagant bolt body is multi-piece, whereas the Mauser is just one piece.

The Mosin bolt body

The Mosin accommodates replaceable bolt heads, similar to the Lee-Enfield Rifle No. 4 (all marks). Unlike the Mauser controlled feed bolt head wherein the Mosin-Nagant cartridge base snaps up under the fixed extractor. As the cartridge feeds out of the magazine, the push feed recessed bolt head's spring-loaded extractor snaps over the rimmed cartridge base as the bolt is finally closed, similar to the Gewehr 88 and Modelo 1891 Carcano or modern sporting rifles like the Remington 700. Both the Mosin and the Mauser rifles feature a blade ejector inset into the receiver. Remove the Mosin bolt by pulling it fully to the rear of the receiver, then squeeze the trigger.

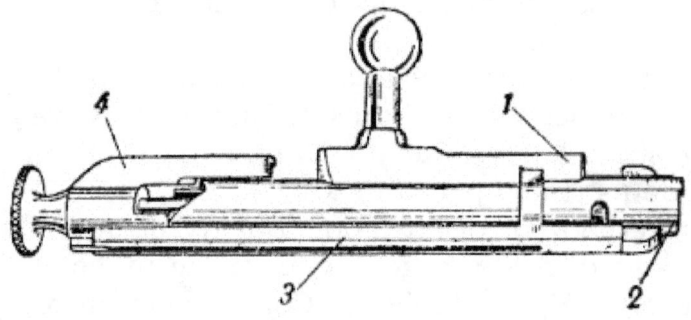

A Mauser's bolt stop lever separates from the trigger. Like the Mauser, bolt lift arc on the Mosin-Nagant measures 90-degrees versus a narrower 60-degree arc on the Lee-Enfield. The Mauser bolt handle positioned at the rear of the bolt body locks behind a solid rear receiver ring. The Mosin bolt handle, similar to the Mannlicher, attaches to a protrusion on the middle of the bolt body. It serves as a bolt guide and locks protruding out of the ejection/loading port in front of a split rear receiver ring. It functions similarly to Mauser's third safety lug. Mosin rifling rotates clockwise (looking down the rifle). There are 4-grooves with a twist of 1 in 9.5 inches.

Jargon Buster

Tryokhlineyka- Three-line

A line represents a unit of measure equal to 1/10th of an inch.

Each one of the three lines denotes a bore diameter of 0.254 cm. (3 X .10 = .30 or 7.62 diameter)

Accordingly, three lines translates to be a 7.62 mm bore diameter for the caliber 7.62 X 54mm.

Tryokhlineyka, besides being a unit of measure, is a Russian language term for the Mosin-Nagant rifle.

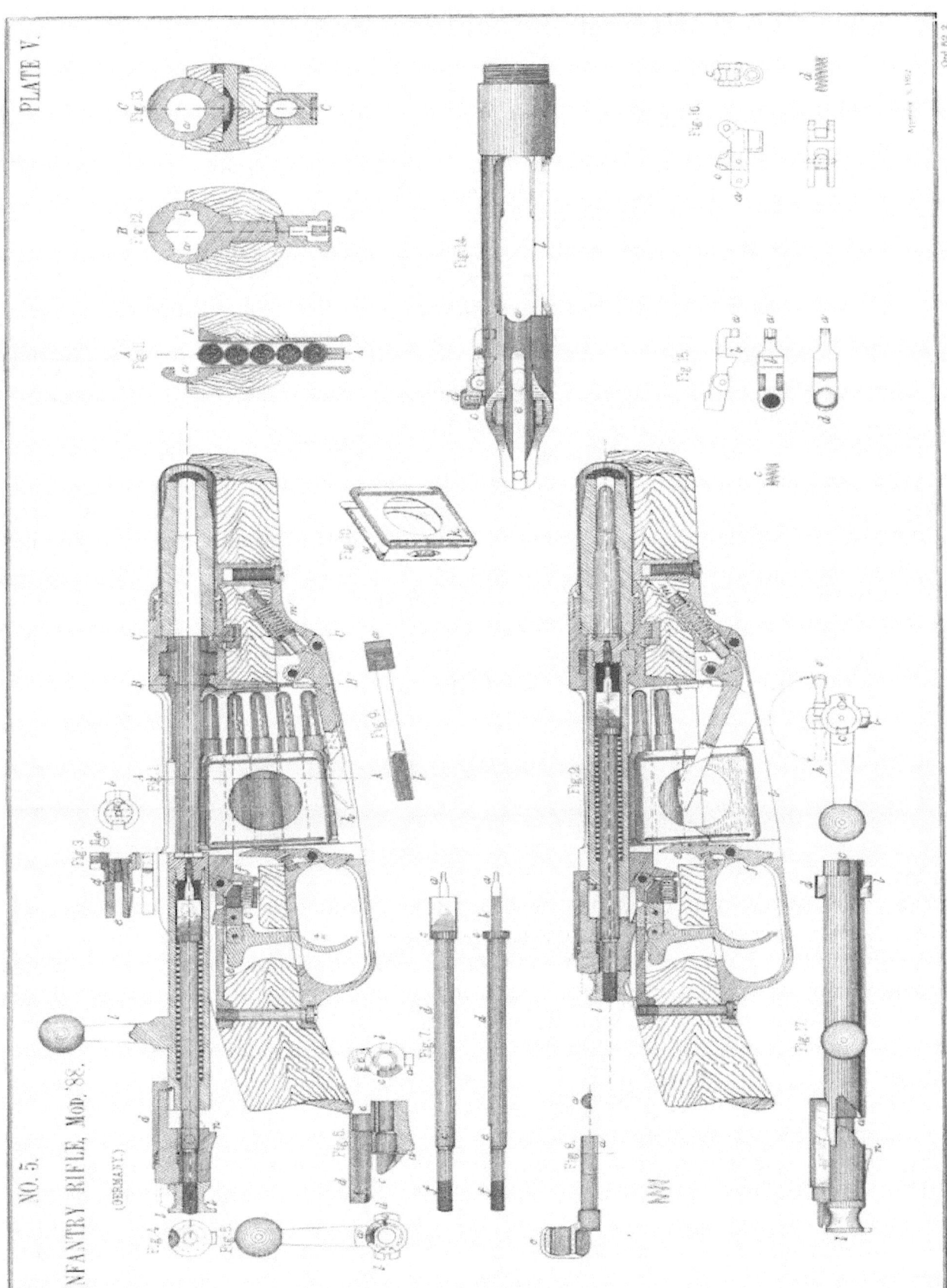

Refinement and Production

The original official designation or the Mosin-Nagant rifle, adopted by the Russian military, is the 3-line rifle, Model 1891. Over the decades since then, several variations have followed. The most common one, the M1891/30, was a modernized 1930 design. Upgrades introduced from Nagant's design included the attachment of the magazine spring to the magazine base plate. With Mosin's original design, the magazine spring did not attach to the base plate. One of the Commission's criticisms was that it was prone to be lost during cleaning. Another salient detail is the form of the stripper clip that held five cartridges, allowing all five to load into the magazine with a push of the thumb. A third detail is the addition of an interrupter. This component was nothing more complicated than a part mounted inside the receiver bolt travel way intended to prevent double feeding, essentially a jam. Mosin's initial rifle lacked an interrupter, which in turn led to numerous Failures To Feed. Borrowed from Nagant's rifle, the shape of the interrupter was slightly changed. Said alteration was subsequently borrowed back by the Commission for the Model 1891 Mosin-Nagant. During the modernization of 1930, the interrupter was further modified from a single to a two-piece design. This reason was as simple as the sea is salt. It was one of the least reliable parts of the action. The only Nagant design features were the stripper clip-loaded cartridges and attaching the magazine spring onto the magazine base plate (in subsequent models). Considering the rifle could be loaded without using a stripper clip, attaching the magazine spring to the magazine base plate qualifies as Nagant's single contribution.

Nagant's Legal Dispute

Despite the failures of Nagant's rifle, he filed a patent suit, asserting he was entitled to the sum the winner was supposed to receive. Nagant applied for international patent protection on the interrupter, even though he had borrowed it lock stock and barrel from Mosin's design. Because Mosin was a Russian army officer could not apply for a patent. A further complication for Mosin, the Russian Government-owned rifle design had the status of a military secret. A scandal erupted. Nagant threatened to no longer participate in trials held in Russia ever again. In an angry response, outraged Russian government officials proposed expelling Nagant from further trials, outraged he had borrowed the design of the interrupter when it fell under the Russian secrecy status given to military inventions. Therefore his patent application violated Russian law.

Nagant was one of the world's few producers not actively engaged by foreign governments and eager to cooperate and share experience and technologies. The Commission begrudgingly paid him 200,000 Russian rubles, a sum equal to the amount Mosin had been awarded when he won the competition. The rifle was never named after Mosin to obviate further conflict with Nagant. This strategy proved to be sound, as in 1895, the Russian army adopted Nagant's revolver as its primary sidearm.

However, because of Nagant's vain attempts to use the circumstances for publicity, the Mosin-Nagant nomenclature appeared in Western literature. The rifle was never called that name in Russia. Applying applicable Russian law from the era, the name is a complete misnomer. None of the details adapted from Nagant's design, removed, would prevent the rifle from firing. Made at the Izhevsk weapons plant, the barrel of the nascent Russian rifle was superior in strength. Another technical point, the long arm that ultimately became known as the Mosin-Nagant, is the Mosin design further amended by Mosin with scant details borrowed from Nagant's design. As it came to pass, production of the Model 1891 began in 1892 at the trinity of ordnance factories of Tula, Izhevsk, and Sestroryetsk Arsenals. In addition, 500,000 rifles were ordered from the French armaments factory, Manufacture Nationale d'Armes de Châtellerault.

Mosin-Nagant Interupter and Spring

In 1889 Tzar Nicolas tasked the Russian army with meeting or exceeding European standards in rifle developments with a reduced bore size and smokeless powder propellant. The new weapons would boast a muzzle velocity exceeding 2,000 feet per second and allow commencing and fighting a land battle at a range of up to two kilometers. New. Mosin-Nagant rifles would replace the Berdan rifles in use by the Russian army.

ABOVE: Old-style, one-piece interrupter-ejector. BELOW two-piece interrupter-ejector.

The Russo-Japanese War 1904 – 1905

The Mosin-Nagant M-1891 The Mosin-Nagant M-1891 rifle's first major blooding would be the Russo-Japanese War (1904-1905). Fought between the Empires of Japan Russia over rival imperial ambitions in Manchuria and Korea. The major military operations were fought on the Liaodong Peninsula and Mukden, southern Manchuria and the seas around Japan, Korea, and the Yellow Sea. By the time the war broke out, approximately 3,800,000 Mosin-Nagant M1891 rifles were built. More than 1.5 million were in the hands of the Russian cavalry and reserves. However, few Model 1891s saw combat in the conflict. Russian units stationed in the far east were still issued Berdan rifles. Several modifications were made to the existing rifles between the initial adoption of the final designs in 1891 and 1910.

Mosin-Nagant rifles and cases of ammunition captured in Fushun during the Russo-Japanese War.

World War I

Russian Imperial infantrymen off to war armed with Mosin-Nagant rifles.

With the start of World War I, simplicity restricted production to the M1891 dragoon and infantry models. In 1915, due to a desperate shortage of armaments, the Russian government ordered a whopping huge 1.5 million M1891s from the Remington Arms Company and another 1.8 million from the New England Westinghouse Company. Remington produced 750,000 rifles before the 1917 October Revolution halted production. When the Treaty of Brest-Litovsk ended hostilities, deliveries to Russia had totaled 469,951 rifles. The new Bolshevik regime of Vladimir Lenin summarily canceled payments to the American companies manufacturing the Mosin-Nagant. Deadbeat Russia had not paid for the order at any time throughout the Great War.

With Remington and Westinghouse teetering on the brink of bankruptcy from the Communists' decision, the United States Army purchased the remaining 280,000 rifles. In the late summer of 1918, American and British expeditionary forces of the

North Russia Campaign, armed with the Army's new Mosin-Nagant rifles, embarked to Murmansk and Arkhangelsk to prevent the large quantities of munitions originally delivered to Czarist forces from being captured by the Central Powers.

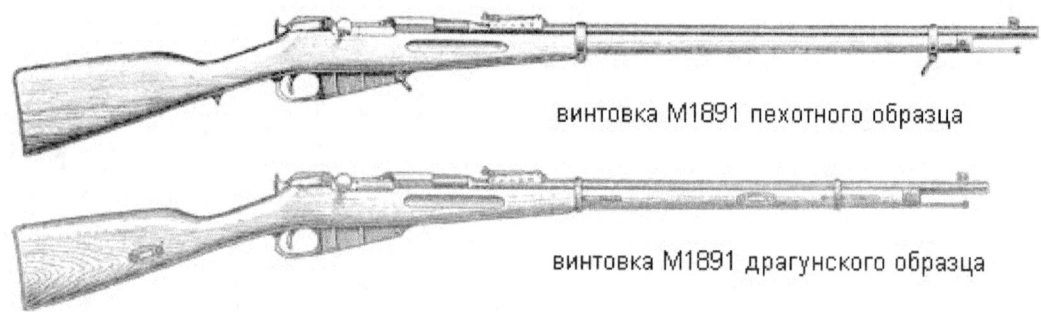

винтовка M1891 пехотного образца

винтовка M1891 драгунского образца

The remaining rifles trained U.S. Army troops. Some equipped the U.S. National Guard, SATC, and ROTC units. Designated as U.S. Rifle, 7.62mm, Model of 1916, they rank among the rarest of American service small arms. Towards the end of World War One, in 1917, the United States government sent 50,000 of its American Mosin-Nagants via Vladivostok to the Czechoslovak Legions trapped in Siberia to secure homeward passage via France. Before World War II, the office of the Director of Civilian Marksman sold New England Westinghouse and Remington Mosin-Nagants to private U.S. citizens. The DCM was the predecessor to the federal government's current Civilian Marksmanship Program. Large numbers of Mosin-Nagants captured by German and Austro-Hungarian forces saw service with both. armies' rear-echelon troops and the Imperial German Navy. Many sold to Finland in the 1920s.

Civil War – 1917 Russian Revolution

During Russia's Civil War, infantry and dragoon versions were still in production, though in dramatically reduced numbers. The rifle deployed to the battlefield in the hands of Bolsheviks, Black Guards, and their enemies, the White Russians (counter-revolutionary forces).

The Winter War 1939-1940

The first Soviet-Finnish War began three months after the outbreak of World War II, with the invasion of Finland on November 30, 1939, It ended three and a half months later. Joseph Stalin, citing concern about a potential attack by the Germans, demanded that Finland create a buffer zone around Leningrad by relocating the border 16 miles back into the Finnish territory. Moreover, Stalin wanted Finland to cede several islands in the Gulf of Finland and grant a 30-year lease on the Hanko Peninsula to construct a Soviet naval base. The Soviets offered a large swath of Russian territory in trade. The Finns, mistrusting Stalin refused. Following a succession of ultimatums and failed negotiations, the Soviet Red Army launched its invasion of Finland with half a million troops. The Winter War had begun. Vastly

outnumbered (one hundred to one), the Finns took advantage of fighting on home turf, opting for a defensive war fought. The weather of 1939 was the coldest winter ever registered. The actual number of Red Army troops frozen to death is unknown. In one battle alone, 10,000 soldiers evacuated due to frostbite.

No big surprise, Finnish troops also suffered a significant number of frostbite casualties. The most common cause for frostbite, on the Finnish side, was footwear, either poor quality civilian boots or military boots sized too small. When proper boots arrived at the front, and troops started to wear captured Russian felt boots, the situation improved.

While the cold winter affected both sides in the fighting, the Finnish troops enjoyed a significant advantage with that country's prewar training. Conversely, the Red Army trained for war on the steppes of Russia, where by Russian standards, winters are mild.

Guerrilla tactics were enhanced by the Finnish winter that bogged down the Soviets, making them easy to spot against snow-blanketed terrain. Led by Marshal Carl Gustaf Mannerheim, Finnish soldiers hunkered down on the Karelian Isthmus, taking cover behind an intricate network of trenches replete with command posts, supply dumps, first-aid stations, kitchens, and latrines. Machinegun emplacements defended against assaults, and deep dugouts sheltered defending troops against bombardment. The Finns repelled repeated Soviet tank assaults. Finnish ski troops took advantage of the Karelian Isthmus rugged landscape to conduct hit-and-run attacks on isolated Soviet units.

The Finnish Army had been trained to fight in Finnish terrain, in Finnish weather. While the skill of skiing was universal among the Finns, it was rare on the Soviet side. Finnish military equipment was entirely appropriate for winter conditions: The infantry tent with the stove and Finnish uniform tunic with the greatcoat. The Red Army also had good winter equipment, with some items valued higher than Finnish counterparts, more particularly the greatcoat and felt boots.

Ultimately the army of Finland was no match for the sheer immensity of the Red Army. In February 1940, Soviet artillery laid down one of the most extensive bombardments since World War I. On its heels, the Soviets Army overran the Finnish defenses dug in on the Karelian Isthmus. The following month, low on ammunition and at the brink of exhaustion, Finland agreed to a peace treaty that forced Finland to cede to the Soviet Union 11 percent of its territory. Finland maintained its independence. During the Second World War/The Great Patriotic War, Finland would once again square off against the Soviet Union. For the Soviets, victory came at a high cost. During three months of fighting, it suffered over 300,000 casualties compared to the Finns' 65,000. Moreover, the Winter War carried significant consequences beyond the conflict. The Red Army's lackluster performance in the Winter War has often been cited as a critical factor in Adolf Hitler's notion that a June 1941 invasion of the Soviet Union be successful.

The Great Patriotic War/World War II

At the beginning of World War Two, known as the Great Patriotic War in the Soviet Union, the Mosin-Nagant 91/30 was the standard issue weapon of Soviet troops. Many millions of these rifles were produced and issued by what was the largest mobilized army in history. In 1935-1936, the battle-proven 91/30 was modified as an expedient measure intended to hasten production. The hex receiver (more accurately, octagonal) was replaced by an easier to manufacture round receiver. When war with Germany broke out, the impetus to produce vast quantities of Mosin-Nagant necessarily led to the further simplification of machining and a falling-off in the qualify of the finish. Wartime Mosins easily identified by tool marks and rough finishing would have failed peacetime quality control inspections. Despite aesthetics, Mosin-Nagant functionality remained intact.

In addition, a 1938 carbine version of the Mosin-Nagant, the M38, came into being using the same cartridge and action as previous Mosins. But its barrel measured 8-inches shorter, reducing overall length to 40-inches. Its forearm was shortened in proportion. The concept was to issue M38 carbines to combat engineers, signal corps, artillerymen, and other troops, whose duties lay behind the front lines. Significantly, the M38 front sight was positioned so a Model 91/30's cruciform bayonet could not be fixed to the muzzle.

An increase in urban combat led to the development of the Model M44 Mosin. In essence, the M44 is an M38 only with a slightly modified forearm and a permanently mounted cruciform bayonet that folds to the side (right) when not fixed for battle. In terms of ergonomics, the M44 was an improvement over the Model 91/30, particularly in an urban warfare setting. Yet few M44s saw combat on the Eastern Front. By 1945, approximately 17.4 million M91/30 rifles were produced.

7.62mm CARBINE, M1938 "MOSSIN-NAGANT" (SOVIET)

M1938 Carbine

M1944 Carbine

Spike Bayonet for M44

Increased Worldwide Use

After The Great Patriotic War ended, the Soviet Union ceased production of the Mosin-Nagant and withdrew them from service in favor of semi-automatic SKS carbines and eventually the AK semi/fully auto rifle. Despite obsolescence, the venerable Mosin-Nagant continued service throughout the Eastern bloc and the rest of the world for decades. During the Cold War, Mosin-Nagant rifles and carbines saw service on many fronts. From Korea and Vietnam to Afghanistan, Africa, and South America, they were maintained as reserve stockpiles and front-line infantry weapons.

During the Cold War, virtually every country that received military aid from the Soviet Union, China, and Eastern Europe used Mosin-Nagants. Middle Eastern nations within the sphere of Soviet influence — Egypt, Syria, Iraq, Afghanistan, and Palestinian fighters — received bolt guns in addition to modern arms. During the Soviet Union's occupation of Afghanistan, from 1979 to 1989, Mosin-Nagants saw action in the hands of both Soviet and Mujahadeen forces.

Its use in Afghanistan continued into the early 21st century by Northern Alliance forces. After the Soviet Union collapsed in 1989-1990, Mosin-Nagants are still commonly found on modern battlefields worldwide. Insurgent forces carried them into battle in the Iraq War and the War in Afghanistan. Mosin-Nagant rifles have been in the hands of rebels in the current Syrian Civil War. in the Second war in Chechnya. Separatists have carried the rifles alongside more modern Russian firearms. In addition, scoped Mosins serve as issue sniper rifles with the Afghan Army, the Iraqi Army, the Finnish Army.

The British Army's iconic Brown Bess Musket (1722-1851)

The Finns used a micrometer sight for sniper training and precision target shooting. In eastern Ukraine's ongoing conflict, both the pro-Russian separatists and pro-Ukrainian forces carry Mosin-Nagants. More than 130 years since its introduction, some otherwise knowledgeable aficionados would assert the Mosin-Nagant is the longest continuously serving rifle in history. They would be wrong. The Mosin-Nagant is not the longest continuously serving combat firearm issued by a government. The Brown Bess musket faithfully served the British Empire from 1720 through about 1865.

Mosin-Nagant Variants

Tula, Izhevsk, Sestroryetsk, Manufacture Nationale d'Armes de Châtellerault, Remington, and New England Westinghouse, produced 37 million- M1891s during its 129-year existence. The Mosin-Nagant has evolved through many variations. We will visit them listed by nation:

Soviet Union – 10	Hungary - 4
Finland – 14	Romania - 3
Poland – 5	China - 1
Estonia - 4	United States of America – 1
Czechoslovakia - 3	

1) TYPE 53 (Cina, 1944)
2) M/24 (Finlandia, Kymen-Laakon-Piiri)
3) M/44 (Romania, 1953-1955)
4) M44 (Polonia, Radom, 1951-1955)
5) M91/59 (URSS, 1930-1959)
6) M1891 (U.S.A., 1915-1919)
7) M1891 "Cosacco" (URSS, 1894-1922)

Mosin-Nagant receiver roll stamps by Lory Tek, licensed under Creative Commons Share Alike license 4.0

IMPERIAL RUSSIA/USSR

Mosin-Nagant Model 1891 Infantry Rifle

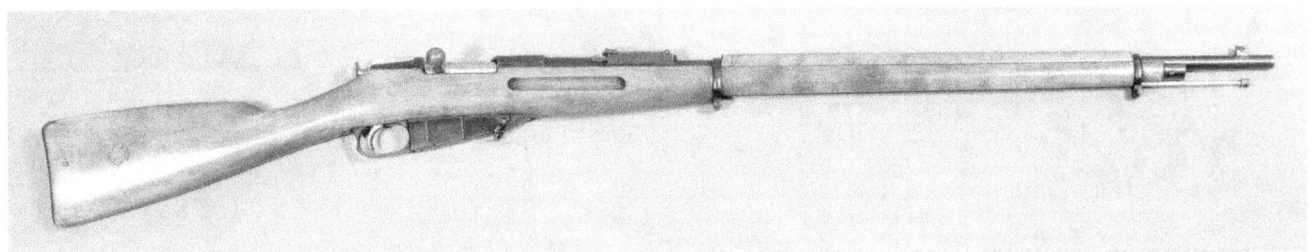

The **Model 1891** Infantry Rifle was the primary weapon of Russian and Red Army infantry from 1891 to 1930. The original weapon lacked handguards and was fitted with sling swivels. It fired a conical nose bullet. Around 1908 a spitzer bullet was adapted and the sight graduations modified, handguards were fitted and sling slots added. Between 1891 and 1910, modifications were made:

- Changed sights.
- The addition of a reinforcing bolt through the finger groove due to adopting a more potent 147-grain pointed spitzer round. New barrel bands were added
- Steel finger rest behind the trigger guard eliminated.

- Slot-style sling mounts replace the traditional swivels.

Mosin-Nagant Model 1891 Dragoon Rifle

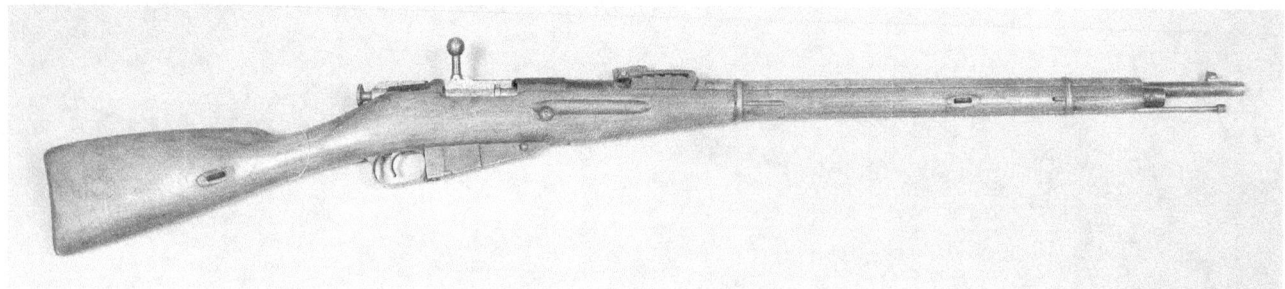

The Mosin-Nagant Model 1891 Dragoon Rifle was the Russian and Red Army infantry primary weapon from 1891 to 1930. Intended for issue to Dragoons (mounted infantry), it measures 64 mm (2.5 inches) shorter and 0.4 kg (0.9 lb) lighter than the M1891. Dragoon dimensions are identical to the later M1891/30 rifle. Most Dragoons were reworked into M1891/30s. Known as ex-Dragoons, and identified by pre-1930 date stamping, small numbers of Dragoon rifles were built from 1930 to 1932 when replaced by the M1891/30. After reworking, it is virtually impossible to distinguish them from purpose-built M1891/30s. Dragoon rifles were marked KAV on the rear sight.

The Cossack Rifle

Produced by Izhevsk Arsenal from 1894-1922, the Cossack Rifle (казачья), appropriately named for being issued to Cossack cavalry, was almost identical to the Dragoon rifle, but sighted without a fixed bayonet, and issued without a bayonet. Know that most Russian military rifles up to World War II were sighted in with the bayonet mounted. All Cossack rifles were stamped KAZ(каз) on the barrel and rear sight. The acronym KAZ is an abbreviation for the Russian word Kazak/Cossack. During the Russian Revolution of 191, the Cossack people mainly sided with the White Russians. Many were wiped out of existence, and their numbers dwindled even more when they took side with Hitler's Nazis during the Great Patriotic war.

Mosin-Nagant M1891 Cossack rifle

A Cossack soldier armed with his Cossack model Mosin-Nagant

Mosin-Nagant Model 1907 Carbine

Model 1907 Carbine: Measures 289 mm (11.4 in) shorter and weighs 0.95 kg (2.1 lb) lighter than the M1891, this carbine was intended for issue to cavalrymen, engineers, signalers, and artillerymen. Stocked nearly to its front sight it could not fix a bayonet. It was produced until 1917, albeit in small numbers.

Mosin-Nagant Model 1891/30

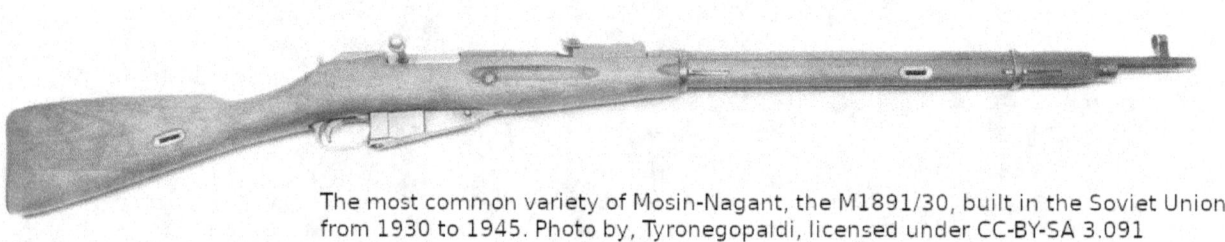

The most common variety of Mosin-Nagant, the M1891/30, built in the Soviet Union from 1930 to 1945. Photo by, Tyronegopaldi, licensed under CC-BY-SA 3.091

Following the Red Army victory in 1924, a committee convened to modernize the rifle that had been in service for three decades. This effort brought the development of the Model 91/30, based on the design of the original dragoon, to fruition. Depot armorers cut barrel length by 3½ inches and dutifully converted rear sight increments from *arshins* into meters. A hooded post front sight replaced a front sight blade otherwise vulnerable to being knocked out of alignment. The bolt received minor modifications but not enough to prevent interchangeability with the earlier Model 1891 and the Cossack Dragoon rifles.

The most numerous of the Mosin-Nagants, this rifle was produced for standard issue to Soviet infantry from 1930 to 1945. Most Dragoon rifles, converted to the M1891/30, were used as sniper rifles in World War II. Early sniper versions featured a 4× PE or PEM scope, a Soviet copy of the Zeiss optical design. Later rifles mounted a smaller, simpler, and easier-to-produce 3.5× PU scope. The scope mounts on top of the receiver.

Mosin-Nagant Model 1938 Carbine

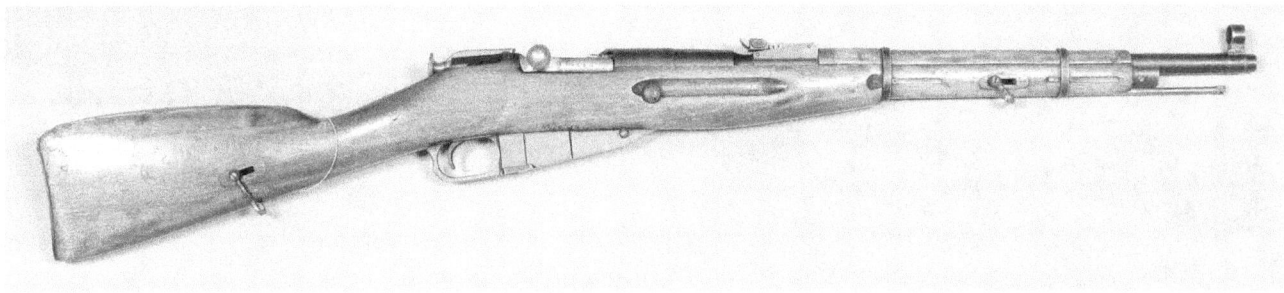

Model 1938 Carbine: The M1891/30-based carbine produced from 1939 to 1945 at the Izhevsk arsenal and in 1940 and 1944 at Tula. It was intended for use by second-echelon and noncombatant troops. Only a small number of M38 carbines were made in 1945 and are understandably highly sought after by collectors. Essentially an M1891/30 with a shortened barrel and stock. The M38 measures 40 inches (1,000 mm) in overall length versus 48 inches for the Model 91/30). Designed so the Model 91/30 bayonet would not fit, this carbine does not accept a bayonet. Note, as a wartime expedient, the Soviets fitted many M38 carbines with M44 stocks. An M38 in the correct M38 stock, commands a premium over an M38 in an M44 pattern stock set. The M44 carbine replaced the M38 in 1944.

Mosin-Nagant M44 Carbine

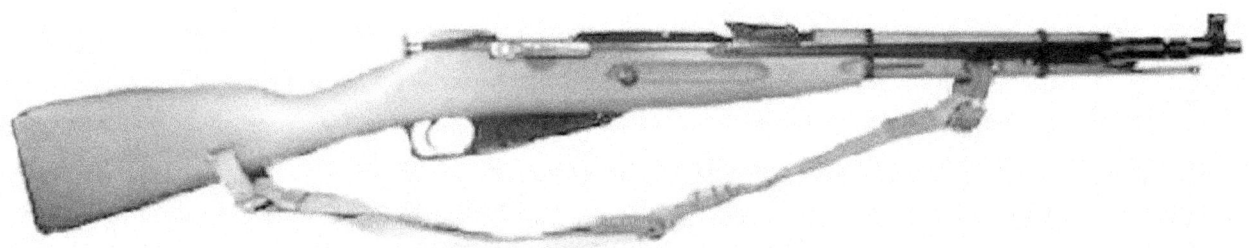

The Model 1944 Carbine was the last of the Mosin Nagant family, derived from the M1891/30. This carbine was introduced into Soviet military service late in 1944. Fifty thousand service-test examples were produced in 1943. This carbine remained in production until 1948. They were made from 1943 to 1948 at the Izhevsk arsenal and only in 1944 at Tula. Specifications are similar to the M1938, with the unique addition of a permanently affixed, side-folding cruciform-spike bayonet. A groove for the folded bayonet is inset into the right side of the stock. Used by the Soviet Union and satellite nations, barrels were counter-bored post-war to clean up damaged rifling near the muzzle.

Mosin-Nagant M59 Carbine

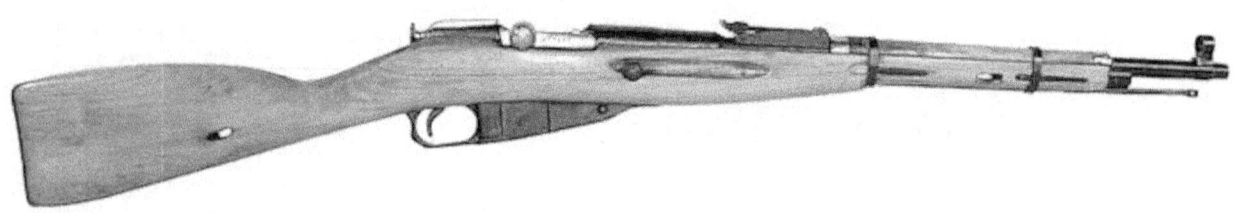

Model 1891/59 Carbine: Commonly referred to as 91/59s, were modified by shortening M1891/30 rifle barrels to carbine length. Rear sight numbers, partially ground, reflect the reduced range. These carbines are near clones of the M38 except for the ground off M91/30 rear sight. Markings on the receiver 1891/59 suggest the carbines were created in or after 1959. It was initially believed either Bulgaria or another Soviet satellite country performed the conversions in preparation for a Western invasion that never came. More recent evidence suggests the M91/59 was produced in Bulgaria from Soviet-supplied wartime production M91/30s. The total production of the 91/59 is uncertain. Estimates range from as low as one million to as high as three million.

The 91/30 Sniper Rifle

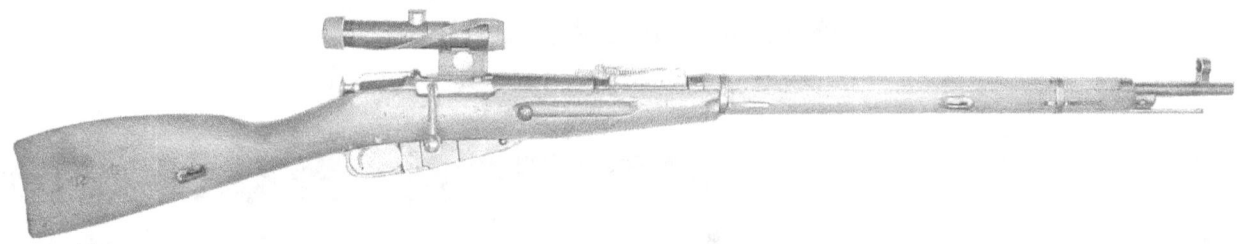

The modified Mosin-Nagant Model 1891/30 was adapted as a sniper rifle from 1932 onwards, initially with German mounts and scopes and later with domestic designs (PE, PEM). From 1942, the sniper rifle version was issued to Soviet snipers with 3.5-power, PU fixed focus scopes. It figured prominently in the bloody urban battles on the Eastern Front. The Battle of Stalingrad made heroes out of snipers Vasili Zaitsev and his comrade Ivan Sidorenko. Mosin-Nagant 1891/30 scoped sniper rifles were revered for being rugged, reliable, accurate, and easy to maintain. On sniper rifles, a longer, bent version replaces the straight bolt handle. Bent at a 90-degree angle the shooter can work the bolt without smacking it into the side of the scope. Its design, based on the Dragoon rifle, came with the following modifications:

- Flat rear sights and rear sight leaf etched in meters instead of *arshinii*.
- A cylindrical receiver replaces the original octagonal/hex receiver. M91/30s built from 1930 to 1936) and converted Dragoon rifles retain an octagonal

receiver. Less common, these rifles are more desirable to collectors.
- A hooded post front sight replaced the blade on previous weapons.

Soviet snipers, Lyudmila Trosky and Nina Slonova.

During the Great Patriotic War, the Soviet Union trained more than a hundred thousand female snipers, about ten percent of all Soviet servicewomen. Moscow's Sniperskya Street is named after a female sniping school that had been located in the area. Eleven female snipers, including the world-famous Lyudmila Pavlichenko, had a headcount of more than 100 enemies. One of Moscow's schools is named after the famous Soviet Kazakh sniper, Aliya Moldagulova, who had a headcount of 78. The school has a small monument to Aliya on its premises.

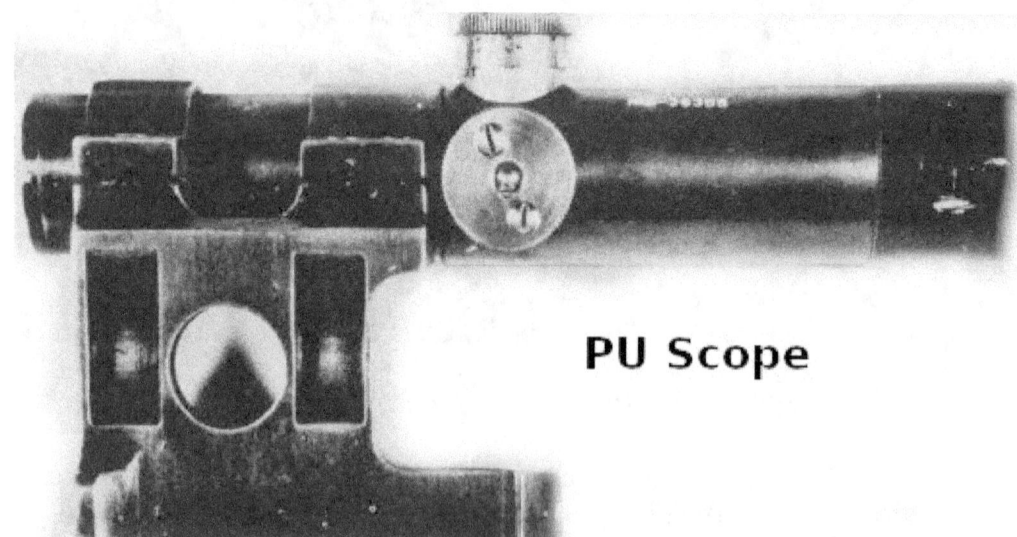

PU Scope

PU-Scoped Mosin-Nagant

PE Scope and Mounts

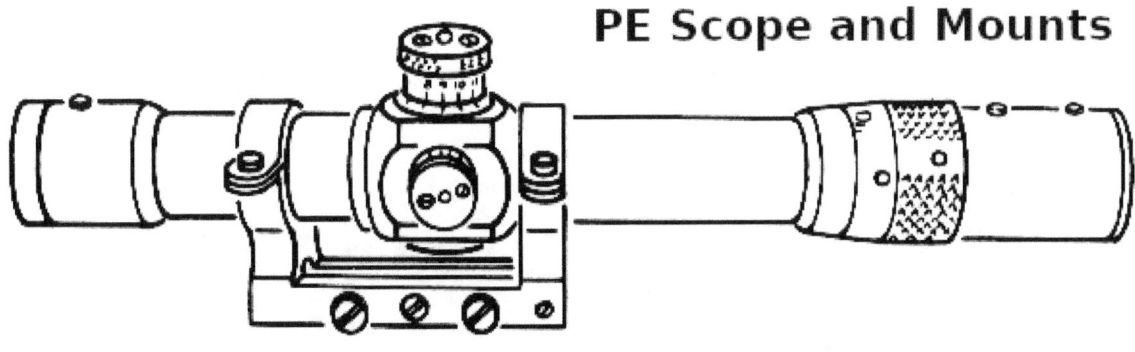

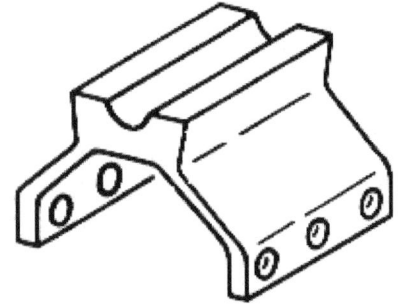

FOR THE HEXAGONAL-SHAPED RECEIVER

FOR THE ROUND-TYPE RECEIVER

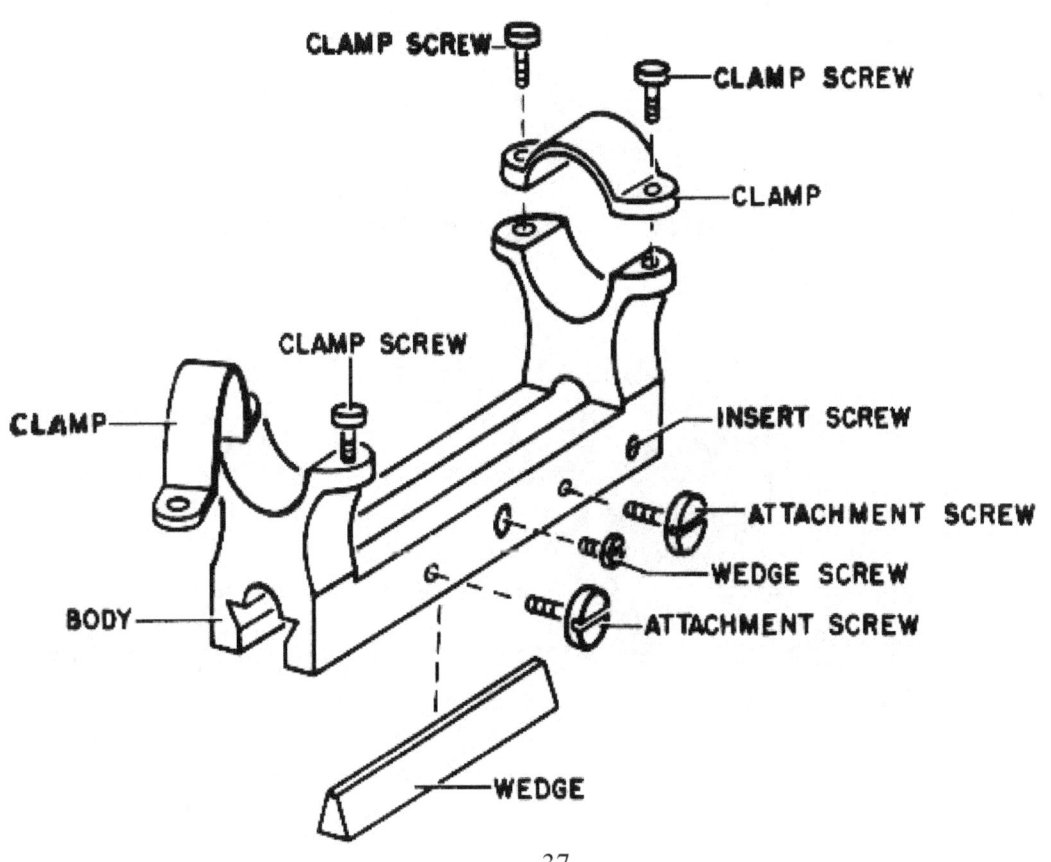

Mosin-Nagant 1891 Obrez

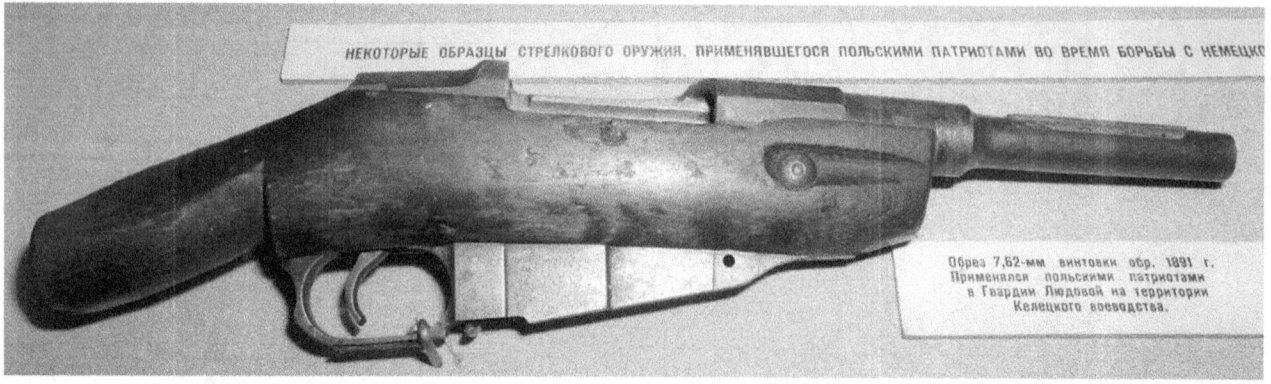

A cutoff Mosin-Nagant M91 used by Polish patriots of the Gwardia Ludowa (People's Guard) in the Kielce Voivodeship. The inscription above the rifle reads: "Some samples of firearms used by the Polish patriots fighting the German Nazi invaders"

Obrez - The sawed-off rifle. During Russia's Revolution and subsequent civil war, revolutionaries, various irregular forces, and common criminals cut down the Mosin-Nagant rifles to pistol size for easier concealment. Most of these crudely fashioned rifle-caliber pistols lacked sights. After the Revolution, the numbers of Obrez bolt-action pistols decreased as the Bolsheviks took over the imperial arsenals and gained access to quantities of Model 1895 Nagant revolvers.. After the Revolution, Obrez bolt-action pistol numbers decreased as the Bolsheviks took over the imperial arsenals and gained access to quantities of Model 1895 Nagant revolvers. Some aficionados his unofficial Mosin variant is perhaps the rarest Mosin of them all and highly prized by collectors.

Ots-48/OTs-48K (short) Sniper Rifles

Developed and manufactured on demand by the Central Design Bureau for Sporting and Hunting Arms (TSKIB SOO), the Tula OTs-48 rifle provides Ministry of Internal Affairs troops and special units with an inexpensive sniper rifle. Also, the gun can be used by civilians for hunting and competition target shooting. This rifle remains in limited use by Russian law enforcement agencies. These rifles were built on military surplus platforms (Mosin-Nagant) stored in the warehouses of the Armed Forces and the Ministry of Internal Affairs. The free sliding barrel is fitted with a short flash suppressor and a front sight post. Its wood buttstock features an adjustable cheek on the buttplate that raises up or down to better fit the shooter. A hinged bipod is positioned near the muzzle.

The OTs-48K variation (K for shortened) includes some aspects of a bullpup configuration. Its non-removable magazine is incorporated in the buttstock behind the pistol grip. The bolt operates by way of a rod linked to it through a pair of hinged levers. OTs-48K features PSO-1 or PKS-07 optics with 7X magnification. Night sights (PKN) or iron sights are optional. Instead of a flash suppressor, a silencer may be attached.

The Republic of Estonia

The Estonian War of Independence, fought in connection with the Russian Civil War during 1918–1920, was a defensive campaign conducted by the Estonian Army and its allies against the Soviet Western Front. After the Estonian War of Independence, Estonia held about 120,000 M/1891s. Sometime later, the Kaitseliit (Estonian national guard) received additional Finnish M28/30 rifles. The Estonian Armory started modernization of M1891 rifles in the late 1920s, fabricating several variants:

The first iteration of a modernized M1891 was the **M1891 moderniseeritud** (M1891 modernized). A total of 15,200 were modernized up until June 1940. Upgrades included:

- Changing the rear sight markings from arshins to meters.
- Adding a new front sight.
- The fitment of a new barrel machined in the Arsenal factory in Tallinn.
- Modifying the original bayonets.

The second model was the **Kütipüss**, an Estonian word that translates as hunter's rifle but more correctly designates a marksman's rifle. The notion was to field a rifle poised between a standard rifle and a sniper's rifle. This model rifle is similar to Finnish 28/30. Every infantry squad had 3 **Kütipüss**, all issued to sharpshooters. About 515-530 were built with the main differences between original M1891s and **Kütipüss** being:

- A new 695 mm/ 27.3" long barrel.
- A thicker barrel (17 mm thick in front versus (original Russian barrel 14,83 mm thick)
- New front and rear sights.
- A front sight protector was also called its Finnish brother püstkõrv (pystykorva in Finnish).
- A new trigger, modified stock to accept new blade bayonet (modified Arisaka bayonet).

KL300, also known as the **Model 1933,** a mere 4,025 were produced. boasting thicker barrels, 2 stage triggers, Mauser-style sling attachment to the butt and its rear sight graduated in metric ranges.

Estonian KL300

The Republic of Finland

In the mid-1920's Tikkakoski machined new barrels for M/91s. Later in 1940, Tikkakoski and VKT built new M/91 rifles. In 1942 VKT ceased production of M/91s in favor of the newer M/39 rifle. Tikkakoski continued building M/91s through 1944. The M/91 qualifies as the most widely issued Finnish rifle in the Winter War and the Continuation War.

A group of Finnish Army non-commissioned officers among rifle racks filled with infantry rifles M/91. *SA-kuva*

Until 1917 Finland had been a Grand Duchy of the Russian Empire. So naturally, it followed Finns had long used the Mosin-Nagant in service with the Tsarist military. The rifle, used in Finland's short civil war, was adopted as the service rifle of the new republic's Army. Finland produced several variants of the Mosin-Nagant founded on Russian-made receivers and later Soviet-made rifles. Captured M91 and M91/30 rifles went to war with minimal modifications. Not surprisingly, the rifle pulled combat duty on both sides of the Winter War and the subsequent Continuation War. SAKO, Tikkakoski, and VKT produced Finnish Mosin-Nagants. Some installed barrels imported from Switzerland and Germany. M/91: Finland achieved independence from

Russia. Vast stores of model 1891 infantry rifles were stockpiled in former Russian military depots situated within the country. The Finnish Army adopted the rifle as its standard weapon and purchased surplus Mosin-Nagants captured on battlefields during World War I from other European nations. Overhauled to meet Finnish Army standards, these rifles were designated the M/91.In the mid-1920´s Tikkakoski machined new barrels for M/91s. Later in 1940, Tikkakoski and VKT built new M/91 rifles. In 1942 VKT ceased production of M/91s in favor of the newer M/39 rifle. Tikkakoski continued building M/91s through 1944. The M/91 qualifies as the most widely issued Finnish rifle in the Winter War and the Continuation War.

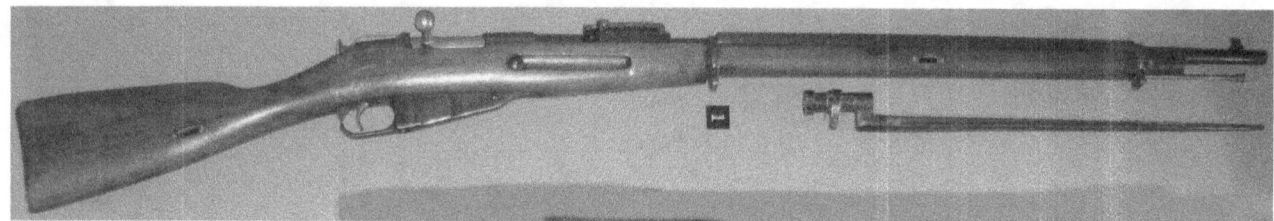

A Finnish 7.62 mm Mosin-Nagant M/91 rifle with spike bayonet.

Finland lumped **Dragoon** and **Cossack** Rifles into a single version, called the **7,62 kiv/91** rv and 762 KIV 91. The M/91rv cavalry rifle was built from captured Russian Model 1891 Dragoon rifles, modified with a sling slot borrowed from the German Karabiner 98a. The original Russian-style sling slots were retained.

M/91: On December 6, 1917, Finland achieved independence from Russia. Vast stores of model 1891 infantry rifles were stockpiled in former Russian military depots throughout the country. A few months later, in August 1918, the Mosin-Nagant M/91 infantry rifle became the official standard rifle issued to Finnish soldiers with the exception of cavalry, bicycle-troops, artillery, and mine-thrower crews. This was a common-sense decision. The infantry rifle M/91 was common in the Finnish arms inventory, and there was no money to purchase other weapons. The Finnish Army adopted the rifle as its standard weapon and purchased surplus Mosin-Nagants captured on battlefields during World War I from other European nations. Overhauled to meet Finnish Army standards, these rifles were designated the M/91.

A complication lie in the fact that many of the m/91s in Finnish hands were poor-quality Imperial Russian, First World War-era production rifles that had deteriorated under poor maintenance regimens and had not been stored correctly. By the early 1920s, a large percentage of those M91s had deteriorated to the point of no longer being fit for service. Note, this was back in the days of corrosive primers, notorious for the way they destroyed bores. No big surprise, barrel corrosion is a big problem. By 1924 the number of Finnish Armed Forces depots rifles in depots suffering from this malady numbered 200,000. To remedy the situation, the Finnish Armed Forces launched a large-scale repair project.

The Finnish Armed Forces lacked equipment for repairing damaged rifle barrels or, for that matter, the money to replace them outright. The sole feasible repair method was either replacing the damaged barrels or relining them with the Salerno method. During World War 1, Italy used the Salerno method to reline 10.4 mm caliber Vetterli M1870/87s, adapting them to fire 6.5 X 52 mm Carcano ammunition. They did this by boring the barrels and installing a rifled inner inside.

Because the Finns had no experience with either method, the Finnish military tested both options. From 1925 - 1927, Weapons Depot 1, located in Helsinki, relined more than 13,000 rifle barrels. Besides boring and inserting a liner, the chamber throat, where it met relined rifling, demanded a touch with a reamer. Concurrent with relining, new rifle barrels were also bought. The Civil Guard, for its part, replaced corroded rifle barrels instead of relining them.

The Finnish attempt to renew corroded barrels by relining proved an abject failure. Some of the relined barrels proved to be of such poor quality they were dangerous. A special committee investigated the matter in 1927, determined; That only 15 % of the relined rifle barrels were good; that 20 - 35 % were unfit for use; and the rest (an estimated 50 - 75 %) needed further repairs. As it came to pass, in 1928, the production of relined rifle barrels was halted.

In a second more detailed inspection in 1930, the reconvened Committee determined that; That only 14 % of the relined barrels were serviceable; That 51 % were unfit for service; and 27 % required further repairs. Assembling rifles with relined rifle barrels stopped as well. Before production of relined barrels stopped, 13,450 infantry rifle M/91, 1,490 rifle cavalry M/91, and 595 Maxim machinegun barrels had been machined. The matter was set to rest. At least until 1938, when the suitability of the relining rifle barrels by way of the Salerno method was re-evaluated. This time, they scored an adequate rating.

During the bleak days of the Winter War, the Finnish military suffered shortages of rifles and other weapons of war. Production was necessarily accelerated, and corners cut to get as many rifles as possible to the front lines. As a result, relined rifle barrels with the worst possible quality rating and other substandard parts big and small were hurried to the assembly line. By May 1940, relined rifle barrels had been used in the repair or manufacture of about 8,000 m/91 infantry rifles.

These eyebrow-raising circumstance changed the legal situation. Previously, in the 1930s, several persons had been sentenced to pay financial reimbursements for their part in the failed relining enterprise. But with previously rejected, relined rifle barrels pulling wartime service, there were no longer grounds for any fines. So in 1940, they were reimbursed, but earlier court sentences were left in place.

Besides rifle barrel repairs, the sights needed to be upgraded to the modern world. Russian rear sight range markings were graduated in *arshins* the Imperial Russian measurement (0.71 meters). Whereas, Finland used the modern metric system. Rear sight settings started at 400 *arshin*- about 284 meters/309 yards. In the real world, which is to say, most engagements occur at a shorter range on battlefields.

Some rifles still fitted with antiquated rear sight tangents were incompatible with the model 1908 ammunition because they had yet to benefit from the 1910 Russian rear sight modification. Old Russian range markings engraved on the left side of the rear sight leaf were denominated with the numbers 4, 6, 8, 10, and 12 (hundreds of arshins).

New metric range settings were engraved on the right side of the rear sight leaf and denominated: 3, 4, 5½, 7, and 8½ (hundreds of meters).

Common Finnish modifications to Mosin-Nagant m/91 rear sights included adding a notch to 150-meter mark on the sight base basic, further requiring a taller front sight. Aimo Lahti, a weapons technician of the Keski-Suomi (Infantry) Regiment, played a significant role in developing the new fore sight and minor improvements on the rifle. These were his first weapons designs. By these methods, from 1919 - 1923, the Finnish military modified the sights of about 66,000 rifles.

M/91 Ulaani Carbine

A Civil Guard unit armed with shortened M/91 Ulaani carbines SA-kuva

While the Finnish Civil Guard had cavalry units, it had few carbines. At the same time Civil Guard owned a substantial number of infantry rifles M/91 with rifle barrel bores in substandard quality. They solved the problem with common sense. Rifles with worn out or damaged barrels were shortened to carbine length: The barrel was cut short, the barrel tip was milled thinner and a ringed front sight base was added. The length of removed barrel varied. About 29cm seems was typical. the front of the stock was shortened to match and modified to work with original nose cap.

These particular shortened carbines were not an official model for the Civil Guard or for the Finnish military. While never common, they appear in early Civil Guard photos and are easily identified due to their combination of carbine-length Mosin-Nagant with rifle rear sight. This carbine is affectionately referred as the Ulaani (Uhlan) carbine, named after a cavalry unit of Kirkkonummi Civil Guard, that fielded these carbines and likely somewhat high profile unit, but apparently not the only Civil Guard unit to be issued with these guns.

Most were shortened by the Civil Guard gunsmiths shop in Helsinki starting year 1920 and this seems to have been a temporary solution with these carbines being commonly replaced already by late 1920's and very few surviving even to mid 1930's.

M/24 - The Lotta Rifle

m/91/24 used by Civil Guard. Another common modification made to infantry rifles m/91 used by Finnish Armed Forces was adding wire swivels for rifle sling. **M24** - Affectionately nicknamed Lotta's rifle by troops who carried it, the Model 24 was the first major Mosin-Nagant upgrade. Lotta's rifle *Lottakivääri* was the namesake of the women's auxiliary of the Civil Guard, the Lotta Svärd, the organization that raised funds to purchase and repair or refurbish 10,000 rifles.

The Finnish Civil Guard (Suojeluskunta) refurbished worn-out Russian M91 rifles, giving life to a new model, the M24. Said rifles had either been acquired from Russia when the Finnish declared independence in 1918 or purchased outright from other countries. Many of these M91 rifles had been in continuous use for 30 years or more. M24 was assembly was completed at Suojeluskuntain Ase-ja Konepaja Osakeyhtiö, the self same Finnish Civil Guard workshop that ultimately came to be known as SAKO. There were three variations on the theme:

Swiss SIG (Schweizerische Industrie Gesellschaft) and a German consortium supplied barrels. Swiss-produced barrels were both standard Mosin-Nagant 1891 contour and a heavier contour designed for improved accuracy. All of the German barrels were heavy-weight. The initial contract for the SIG-produced barrels, let on April 10, 1923, was for 3,000 barrels machined to the original Model 1891 barrel contour.

The following year a subsequent contract was let for an additional 5,000 heavier barrels, stepped at the muzzle to fit the standard Mosin-Nagant spike bayonet. Starting in 1924 and running to 1926, the German contracts were for heavy, stepped barrels. There were two contracts: The first for 5,000 barrels and the second for 8,000 barrels. Bohler-Stahl is roll-stamped on the underside of the chamber of German-made barrels. All Model 24s marked with the Civil Guard logo have three fir tree sprigs over a capital S. Model 24s are equipped with a coil spring around the trigger pin to improve trigger pull and accuracy.

Suojeluskunta sought bids for the replacement barrels from companies in Switzerland and Germany in 1923. The initial contract was awarded to the Swiss firm Schweizerische Industrie-Gesellschaft of Neuhausen am Rheinfalls, SIG. An additional contract to a German arms consortium made up of Venus Waffenfabrik and Romrwerke AG was awarded in 1924. SIG barrels were marked on the right of the chamber just above the stock: Schweiz-Industrie Gesellschaft Neuhausen. German barrels bear the mark Bohler-Stahl under the chamber.

The first order of 3,000 Swiss SIG barrels was dimensionally identical to those on the M91. The remainder of SIG barrels and the German manufactured barrels are heavier. Barrel diameter increased marginally (by approximately 1mm) for improved accuracy, with a step near the muzzle accommodating the standard bayonet. M24 barrels are undated, featuring the Finnish Civil Guard crest roll stamped don top of the chamber: The letter-S topped with three fir sprigs enclosed within a shield.

The forestock barrel channel was deepened to fit the larger diameter barrel. Similarly, the handguard was inletted deeper. An improved trigger added a coil spring to take up the slack and improve trigger pull. These design changes were instituted in mid-1925. Many rifles were fitted with a cross-bolt through the forestock. Positioned just behind the nose cap to retain the front barrel band, this left the barrel band loose, eliminating a pressure point on the barrel. The happy result: Better accuracy. Eventually, Finland eliminated the modification, securing loosened barrel bands with small wood screws.

M24 production ceased in 1928, But the M24 remained in service until the guard disbanded in 1944, its arms transferred to the regular army. Due to the low numbers of M24 manufactured and high loss rates during the Winter War, Continuation War, and Lapland War, collectors highly prize it.

The **Model 27,** the Finnish Army's virtual complete reworking of the Model 1891, was nicknamed Pystykorva (literally spitz) due to its foresight guards. The 1891 receiver and magazine were retained with a new shorter-length heavy-weight barrel added. The receiver and bolt were modified. Sights were modified. Wings fitted to the bolt connecting bars ride on slots machined into the receivers. In the early days, 1891 stocks were cut short, and barrel channels opened to accommodate a heavier, larger diameter barrel.

A new nose cap and barrel band were fitted. A new bayonet was issued. The modified stocks broke when soldiers practiced bayonet fighting or firing with a fixed bayonet. In the mid-1930s, these problems and others resulted in a slow-down of production. Ultimately solutions were engineered. Existing stocks of rifles were modified. The Model 27 was the Finnish Army's primary battle rifle in the Winter War.

M/27rv This is a cavalry carbine version of M27 (rv short for *ratsuväki*- literally mounted force). M/27 were made and issued the elite Finnish cavalry units. Due to heavy use throughout the Winter and Continuation Wars, nearly half were lost. Most surviving examples were deemed beyond repair and scrapped. About 300 are still in existence, making it the rarest out of all Finnish Mosin-Nagant models.

M/28

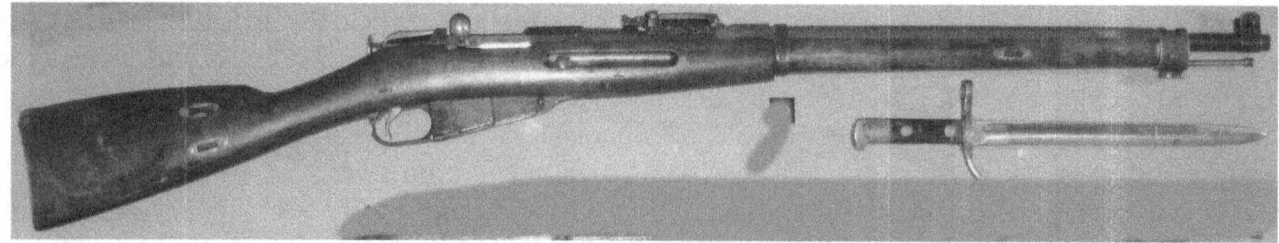

Finnish 7.62 mm rifle M/28 with M/28 Sk bayonet.

The **M/28** variant, designed by the White Guard, differs from the Army's M/27 in that its barrel band design is one piece compared to the M/27's hinged band. Perhaps more significant is its improved trigger design. Barrels for the M/28 barrels were purchased from SIG and later from both Tikkakoski and SAKO.

M/28-30

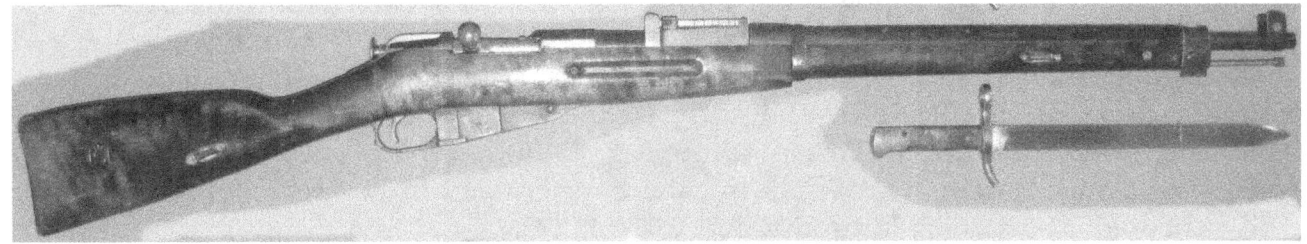

Finnish 7.62 mm rifle M/28-30 with M/28-30 bayonet.

An upgraded variant of the M/28, its most noticeable modification is its new rear sight design. This same sight was used in the following M39 rifle only exception being "1.5" marking for the closest range to clarify it for users.

Trigger action improved by adding a coil spring to minimize long travel. The later M39 does not benefit from this improvement. The magazine was modified to prevent jamming. Magazines were stamped on the right side with HV, short for *Häiriö Vapaa*, meaning Jam Free.

M/28-30's metal sleeve in the fore-end of the hand-guard reduces barrel harmonics. It makes barrel-stock contact more consistent between shots and during environmental changes such as moisture and temperature. Later M39 does not benefit from this upgrade.

In addition to military duty, SAKO manufactured approximately 440 M/28-30 rifles for Helsinki's 1937 World Shooting Championships.

M/28-30 model, serial number 60974, used by Simo Häyhä, a famous Finnish sniper. Before World War II, Civil Guards shot the M28/30 in competition, as did Simo Häyhä. Therefore, rifles were built very well, with the highest grade barrels available and carefully matched headspace. As of 2002, Häyhä's rifle was held in the repository at PKarPr (Northern Karelia Brigade) museum until the Finnish Army moved it to an undisclosed location.

M/91-35: Proposed by the Finnish Army to replace both its M/27 and White Guard's M/28 and M/28-30 rifles. The White Guard objected to this proposal considering the M91/35 to have poor accuracy and excessive muzzle flash. It was never adopted, instead of being supplanted by the M/39.

Finnish M39

In assembling M39 rifles, Finnish armorers re-used octagonal receivers that dated back as far as 1894. Finnish rifle receivers (Russian, French, or American-made) are stamped with a boxed SA rollstamp. Many of its other parts were produced in foreign countries, with barrels rifled in Finland, Switzerland, Austria, Belgium, and Germany. The Finns manufactured visually distinctive three-piece finger splice stocks for their Mosin-Nagant rifles.

In addition, the rifle was distributed to the Iberian peninsula to aid Republican anti-Franco forces in the Spanish Civil War. Spanish Civil War Mosins are identifiable by their wire sling hangers inserted in the forearm and buttstock slots to accommodate the Russian dog collar slings that accept Western European-style rifle slings. The vast number of Finnish Rifles were built by SAKO, *Tikkakoski Oy,* or VKT (*Valtion Kivääritehdas,* States Rifle factory. After wars end, *Valtion Metallitehtaat* (Valmet), State Metalworks. By the end of the Winter War, a mere ten rifles were built. But after the Winter War, a whopping 96,800 were produced and saw duty during the Continuation War. Small numbers assembled from spare parts in the late 1960s through 1970 boosted production to 102,000.

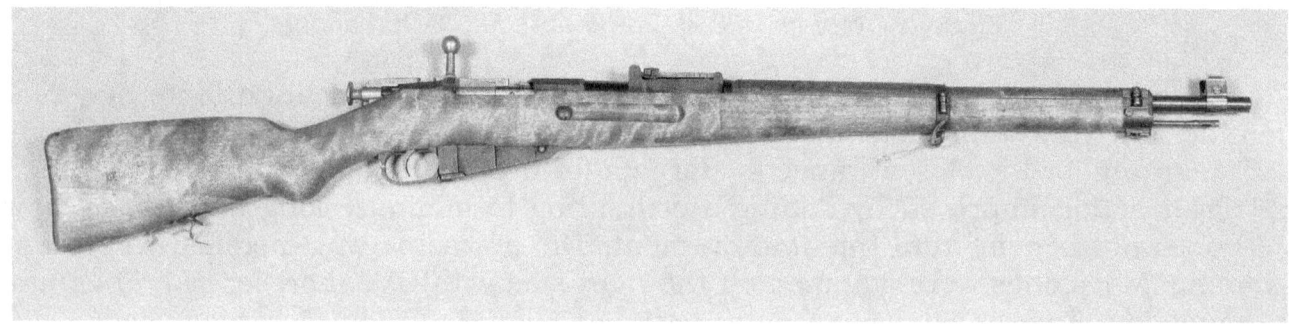

The **M/39**, affectionately nicknamed the *Ukko-Pekka,* after Finland's former President *Pehr Evind Svinhufvud.* The model was a compromise between the Army and White Guard factions, adopted to standardize Mosin-Nagant production. The M/39 mainly derived from the M28-30 included alterations proposed by the Army. The M/39 incorporated a semi-pistol grip stock. Though early examples were fitted with typical Mosin-Nagant straight stocks.

Deliveries of M/39 rifles by September of 1945

Year	Sako	AV3	Total
1941	16000	0	16000
1942	4000	8000	12000
1943	20000	17646	37646
1944	13500	4683	18183
1945	6500	0	6500
Total	60000	30329	90329

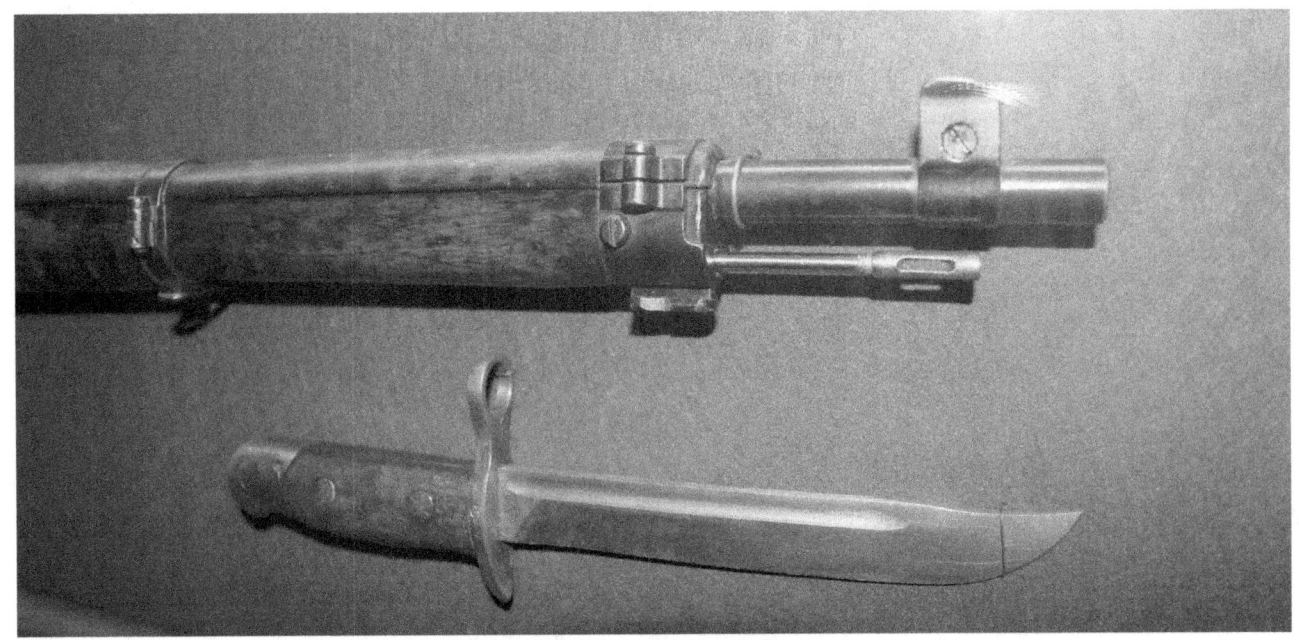

Muzzle and bayonet of the Finnish infantry rifle m/39 Ukko-Pekka.

M/30: In 1943 and 1944, Tikkakoski built high-quality Model 1891/30 rifles. Designated the M/30, it sported new barrels and parts and pieces from the almost 125,000 1891/30s captured during the Winter and Continuation Wars and 57,000 battlefield pickups bought from the Germans in 1944. Most of which were only suitable as parts donors). Both one- and two-piece stocks were produced, and either Soviet globe or Finnish blade front sights fitted.

M/56: An experimental 7.62×39mm variation.

M/28-57: A biathlon 7.62×54mmR variation.

M/28-76: Produced in two different versions by the Finnish Army, a special marksmanship and target rifle for continued training and competition built from modified M/28-30 and M/39 rifles.

Tkiv 85: A modern marksman/sniper rifle founded on original Mosin-Nagant receivers built by Valmet and the Finnish Defence Forces (FDF) Asevarikko 1 (Arsenal 1) in Kuopio.

The 7.62 TKIV 85, short for 7.62 Tarkkuuskivääri 85 (7.62 sniper rifle 85), with a Zeiss Diavari ZA 1.5–6×42 telescopic sight

Finland's Simo Häyhä

As a point of history, it is worth noting now Finland's Army also employed the highly vaunted Mosin-Nagant sniper rifle, successfully with their fabrications and captured Soviet rifles. An example is Finland's a sniper who killed 505 Soviet soldiers, many of whom fell victim to shots fired from his Finnish M/28-30 Mosin-Nagant rifle. Curiously, Häyhä did not scope his Mosin but instead relied on iron sights. In interviews, Häyhä asserted Soviet-designed scopes and mounts required a shooter to raise his head too high, increasing the odds of being spotted and knocked off.

Czechoslovakia

VZ91/38 Carbine: Similar to the M91/59, an M38-style carbine modified by shortening Model 1891 Infantry, Dragoon, and Cossack rifles. The reason for their genesis is murky. Like the M44, it boasts a bayonet groove cut into the right side of the stock, despite any evidence that the VZ91/38 design ever fixed a bayonet. The front sight's wide base is similar to post-WWII M44's.

VZ54 Sniper Rifle: Founded upon the M1891/30, boasting the appearance of a modern sporting firearm. The VZ54 mounts a Czech 2.5 power scope and unique rear sight. It borrows Mauser's locking screws and the 98k front sight hood.

VZ54/91 Sniper Rifle: An updated version of the VZ54 Sniper Rifle. The VZ54/91 features an adjustable biathlon stock with an adjustable comb and butt plate. A forearm rail accepts adjustable sling swivels and a bipod. A Soviet manufactured PSO-1 scope used on the SVD Dragunov sniper rifles mounts on a side plate. It retains front and rear sights of the VZ54.

The People's Republic of China

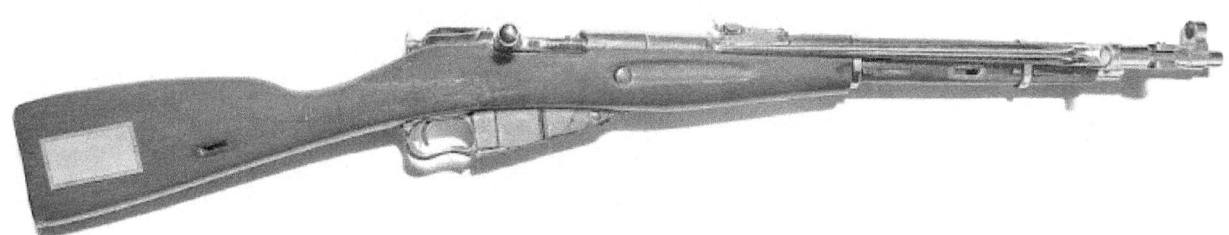

Chinese Type 53 Carbine

The **Type 53**, a license-built post-war Soviet M1944 carbine, did not show an abundance of markings or variations. Neither was it known to have been produced at any Arsenal other than /26\, Jianshe. The Soviet Union sent advisers and tooling to the famous Arsenal /26\.\

After production began, the Chinese tagged it as Type 53 after its first year of build. Production seems to have ended in 1961, but this is not confirmed. The latest recorded date for a T53 is 1961, and a Vietnam War bring back souvenir from an American soldier. The T53 weighs more than a standard 91/30 due to the heft of its attached bayonet. T53s are less collectible and less valuable than authentic Russian M44 due to the mistaken belief that the Chinese made weapons of a lesser quality than the Russians. This is false. Many carbines imported to the USA are constructed of local Chinese parts and surplus Soviet parts, giving rise to the debate about when this mixture occurred. Type 53s are encountered with or without a permanently attached folding bayonet. The former is more common.

From 25 June 1950, until the armistice was signed on 27 July 1953, the Korean War, alternatively known as the Fatherland Liberation War, was fought between North and South Korea. A United Nations coalition headed by the United States fought for South Korea. China, assisted by the Soviet Union, fought for the North.

Given its initial production date of late 1953, few T53s ever saw service in the conflict, with either the North Korean or Chinese soldiers.

The Chinese Type 53 carbine served extensively with the People's Liberation Army from 1953 until the early 1960s, when the PLA transitioned to the Chinese Type 56 carbine (SKS) and the Chinese Type 56 assault rifle (AK47).

Many Type 53 carbines were issued to the People's Militia in China, who used Type 53 until 1982 when replaced with modern weapons. T53s also went to North Vietnam. During the 1960s and 1970s, many landed in the hands of the National Liberation Front in South Vietnam, the Viet Cong, and Cambodia's Khmer Rouge in Cambodia. During the 1960s Chinese gifted significant numbers of Type 53 carbines to Albania as military aid. During the late 1990s, some of those carbines armed the Kosovo Liberation Army.

Hungary

After the Second World War ended, Hungary's military was limited to 25,000 members. The military's only weapons were: 10,600 35M and 43M Mannlicher rifles, 6250 39M, 43M, and MP-40 Machine Pistols, plus a sprinkling of 1274 pistols chambered in different calibers. Hungary's military purchased a limited number of Soviet firearms, including M91/30 and M44 Mosin Nagants, PPSh41 machine pistols, and TT33 pistols.

By 1948 the Warsaw Pact was pressuring Hungary to buy the license from the Soviet Union to manufacture Mosin Nagants and other Soviet weaponry. Production was limited to quality copies of the Soviet Model 1944 carbine, alternatively known in Hungary as the 48.M (48 Minta). Hungary's Warsaw Pact issued factory marking is stamped on most parts of the rifle.

The **Gyalogsági Puska 48.M** (48.Minta) rifles are high-quality 1891/30 variants, built by the FEG (Fémáru Fegyver és Gépgyár), Budapest. Built from 1949 to 1955, these weapons are characterized by their high-quality finish and all parts being marked with an 02 stamp. Stock furniture is beech wood. The standard military finish is oil with a low sheen. The buttstock is marked with the 02 country code and an encircled B representing Budapest.

On the top of the chamber, the barrel is stamped with the Communist Hungarian Rákosi Crest: A crossed hammer replete with a stalk of wheat, surmounted by a 5-point star and flanked on both sides by wreaths of wheat. Leaf sight graduations range from 100 to 1000 meters. The permanently mounted bayonet is a socket-type folding spike blade.

Femaru-Fegyver es Gepgyar (FEG) manufactured an M1891 sniper version based on the 48 in the 1950s. This model saw extensive duty with the North Vietnamese Army (NVA) during the Vietnam War.

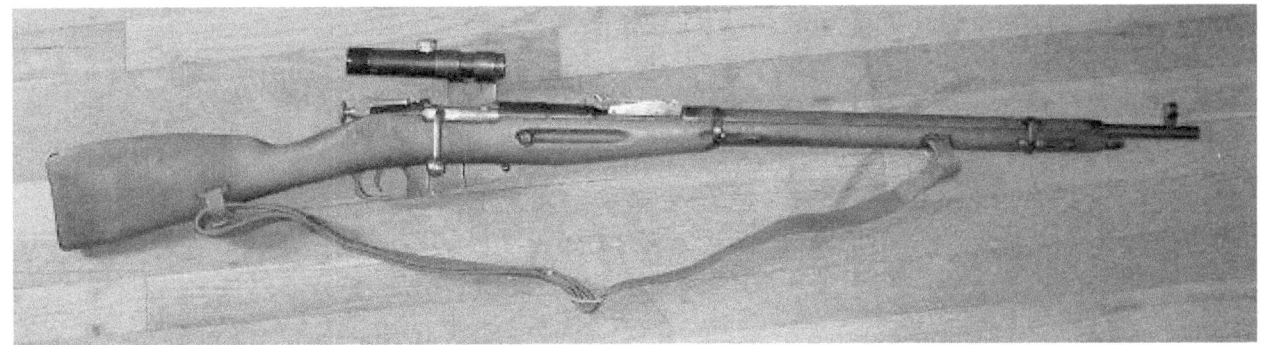

Mosin-Nagant M/52 sniper rifle

The **M/52** is a direct copy of the vintage Soviet Model 1891/30 sniper rifle. Identifying features include:

- Hungarian M/52 rifle replete with PU 3.5× optics.
- Darkly blued steel and high-quality machining.
- 02" stamped on every component of the gun, identifying it as manufactured in Hungary
- **M44 Pattern**: Domestically produced version of post-war pattern Soviet M44 Carbine marked "02"

Romania

Triangular-shaped markings, sometimes enclosing an arrow, stamped on many components of the rifle. On the top of the breech, three letter-Rs flanked by crossed stalks, leaves pointing outwards. Year of manufacture stamps are prominent. The adjustable trigger assembly is unique in the Romanian 91/30 and is not interchangeable with other Mosins.

M44 Pattern: Domestically produced version of post-war Soviet M44 Carbine during the years. Overshadowed in prestige by Soviet and Polish M44's, surpassed in production numbers by China & Hungary, the Romanian M44 is an exciting and obscure Mosin-Nagant variant. Production began in 1953 and ended in 1955. With a mere 70,000 units built, it is one of the rarest Mosin Nagant variants.

Most surplus Romanian M44's are mix-masters built with Soviet and Communist Block components. Compelling evidence that leftover parts find their way into their M44 production. Romanian M44 proof markings are nearly identical to those on Soviet Izhevsk M 44s. The Izhevsk proof mark is an arrow inside a triangle. The Romanian proof mark is an arrowhead in a triangle. So arrow versus arrowhead. The Romanian M44 upper barrel shank proof mark is a wreath with RPR (Romanian People's Republic). Once again, similar in design, Izhevsk shows a Wreath with Hammer and Sickle. This similarity makes it easy to mistake a Romanian for Izhevsk. That said, a Romanian stock's letter-C set in a diamond proof makes them easy to identify. Another telltale, the furniture shows little to no wood grain, lending a plain look. A heavy coat of shellac is typical. The blued finish is deep and lustrous.

Romanian M44 Pattern Production Numbers

1953- 2,000 – 3,000
1954- 36,000
1955- 31,00

Suppressed M44 Pattern Domestically-produced adaptation of the M44, replete with a long integral suppressor and the same LPS 4×6° TIP2 telescopic sight, used on the PSL rifle. Small numbers were modified for issue to the USLA - an elite 1953 to 1955 counter-terrorism unit of the Security.

M91/30 Pattern: Domestically produced during 1955.

Some Mosin-Nagants were **INSTRUCTIE,** held in reserve for a secondary line of defense in the event of an invasion. Typically, the Instructie mark, but not always, was accompanied by a broad red band painted on the butt stock Some aficionados do not consider these weapons to be safe to fire. But most, while admittedly well worn and in a somewhat neglected appearance, seem to be in good working order.

EXERCITIU rifles were intended for use in the event of an extreme national emergency, i.e., a foreign invasion. A black-striped buttstock is a prominent feature of Exercitiu rifles. An Ex stamped on the receiver is the abbreviation for Exercitiu. They will not fire: The firing pin is clipped, and parts critical to proper function are missing.

Poland

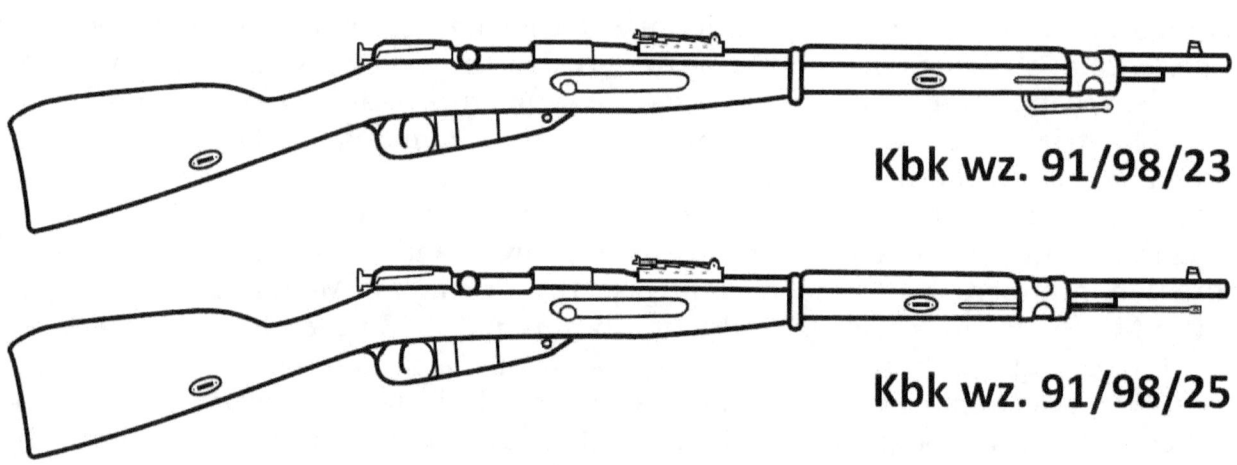

Created in the Second Polish Republic by modifying Russian Mosin M1891 rifles to the 7.92×57mm Mauser cartridge. Line art by, Sumek101, licensed under the Creative Commons Attribution-Share Alike 4.0 International license.

Karabinek wz. 91/98/23 Carbine, Mark 1891/1898/1923 (kbk wz. 91/98/23), a Polish modification of the Mosin-Nagant M1891 rifle shortened from rifle to carbine and converted 8 X 57 mm Mauser cartridge.

The carbine, introduced as an interim weapon in the 1920s, continued in use until Poland fell at the start of World War II. After that, some were used by Germany.

During the 1919-1921 Polish-Bolshevist War, Poland captured huge numbers of all types of Mosin rifles from Izhevsky Zavod, Tula Arms Plant, Sestroretsk Plant, and American-made rifles by Remington and New England Westinghouse. By 20 January 1919, 20% of the rifles used by the Polish Army were Mosins. Despite losses during the war, in 1922, there were still more than 120,000 Mosin-Nagant rifles in Polish service.

Although in the early 1920s, the army adopted the Mauser-based Kb wz. 98a rifle as its standard weapon. Initial supplies were scant so captured Mosin rifles were converted to carbines. Centralna Składnica Broni, Warsaw and ARMA Ltd., Lwów (modern Lviv) converted some 77,000 Mosin rifles to the new standard between 1924 and 1927. SePeWe dispatched some 3,000 unmodified Mosins to the Spanish Republic during the Spanish Civil War aboard SS Cieszyn. The remainder sold on the civilian market.

Modifications included:

Re-chambering to 7.92×57mm Mauser and magazine to feed modified for the rimless cartridge
Barrel over-bored or outright replacing if needed
Barrel shortened by about 20 cm (7.9 in)
Barrel mounting shortened
Russian spike bayonet mount replaced with a Polish and German compatible mount.
  Lock and bolt group modified
  Firing pin shortened
  Sights modified to match 7.9 ballistics
  Stripper clip modified to accept 7.9 rounds
  Straps added to butt stock and cradle

Polish Variants

The original **wz. 91/98/23** utilized the original Mosin-Nagant spike bayonet. In 1925 the design added a bayonet mounting bar allowing Polish and German knife bayonets used with Mauser rifles to be mount. The Seitengewehr 84/98, Bagnet karabinowy wz. 22, wz. 24 and wz. 25. Introduced as the **Karabinek wz. 91/98/25**, a year later, modified to include a two-piece ejector/interrupter, similar to Mauser rifles. The Army accepted the final version as Karabinek wz. 91/98/26.

Issued to the 20th Infantry Division's 80th Infantry Regiment, the kbk wz 91/98/23 was the standard service carbine of the Polish cavalry, mounted artillery, and military police. By 1929, active units replaced it with the wz 29 carbine. The remaining guns were supplied to the State Police, Border Guard, and certain units of the National Defence. With World War II (German and Soviet invasion of Poland), 76,400 rifles remained in Polish inventory. Most were destroyed during the war.

wz. 91/98/23m Converted to the 7.92 x 57mm Mauser cartridge, its magazine modified to feed rimless cartridges. It utilized the Model 1891s spike bayonet.

wz. 91/98/2 Converted to the 7.92 x57mm Mauser cartridge, its magazine modified to feed rimless cartridges, and a bayonet mounting bar added to fix the Mauser 1898 bayonet.

wz. 91/98/26 Converted to the 7.92x57 mm Mauser cartridge, with its magazine modified to feed rimless cartridges. A mounting bar allowed fixing the ubiquitous Mauser 1898 bayonets. The modified two-piece ejector/interrupter was similar to Mauser pattern rifles.

wz. 44: Domestically produced versions of post-war pattern Soviet M44 Carbine prominently marked with the Polish Circle 11.

Mosin M1891 rifle	Versus	Karabinek wz. 91/98/26
7.62×54mmR	Cartridge	7.92×57mm Mauser
1,306 mm (51.4 in)	Length	1,000 mm (39 in)
4.06 kg (9.0 lb)	Loaded weight	3.7 kg (8.2 lb)

The United States of America

U.S. Rifle, 7.62 mm Model of 1916.

The Imperial Russian Army desperately needed rifles lots of rifles. Russian government ordered 1.5 million M1891 rifles from Remington Arms and another 1.8 million from New England Westinghouse and a goodly amount of ammunition. The contract was made for 1.8 Million Mosin-Nagant 91s at the price of $27.50 per rifle, today's equivalent of $667. Czar Nicholas II had approached George Westinghouse due to a good working relationship with American managers of the Westinghouse electric power plant in St. Petersburg.

New England Westinghouse Built Mosin-Nagants

New England Westinghouse was founded in East Springfield, Massachusetts, on May 16th, 1915. World War One had started the year previous. Contrary to popular belief, New England Westinghouse was not a division of Westinghouse Electric Corporation, Pittsburgh, Pennsylvania, famous for bringing electricity to American factories and homes worldwide. But instead, it was incorporated as a separate entity for the sole purpose of building rifles for Tsar Nicolas II's Imperial Russian Army. The

Springfield area was chosen for the Russian war effort because it was the center of arms production in the United States.

Westinghouse Meriden Fire Arms Factory

Previous to its Russian war effort order, New England Westinghouse had never produced so much as a single firearm. So naturally, it followed the company needed a building, tooling, and machinery. In June 1916, it purchased the factory and machinery of the Meriden Fire Arms Company in Meriden, Connecticut, and retooled to make the Mosin-Nagants. A month later, they also purchased the J. Stevens Arms and Tool Company in Chicopee Falls, Massachusetts, including the Stevens-Duryea Automobile company in East Springfield, Massachusetts. The J. Stevens Arms factory was retooled rifles and was soon producing 6000 Mosin-Nagant rifles a week. Destiny would come to wept. Many remained undelivered before the outbreak of the October Revolution.

Remington-Built Mosin-Nagant's

Remington UMC received a down payment of $7,500,000 and used the money to build the Bridgeport Rifle Works, purchase both machinery and raw materials. Remington UMC labored for five months, from March to August 1915, constructing the immense Russian rifle plant. Completed in the fall of 1915, it boasted one million square feet under a roof on four floors, the largest factory ever built in the United States all at one time. Thirteen parallel buildings stood five stories high, duly separated so an explosion in one sector would not start a chain reaction and level the entire plant. Buildings were linked by a central, five-story corridor half a mile long, boasting 80 acres of floor space.

The Remington Arms Company Bridgestone factory circa 1916.

The gargantuan size and capacity of the factory invited a 200,000 rifle contract from the French government for Mdl 1907-15 Berthier rifles chambered in caliber 8mm Lebel. Delays in deliveries of rifle-making machinery, as well as labor problems, stymied deliveries. Lack of proper equipment, and skilled workers, hurt Remington's build quality. In 1916 French military inspectors rejected Remington Berthiers due to rifling and chamber dimensions being out of specification. Labor strikes further added to delays, resulting in Russian Mosin-Nagant contract cancellations.

Many hundreds of thousands of rifles were fabricated in late 1916 and into 1917. Remington records show 4,000 and 4,200 Russian rifles were built per day, for an astounding 100,000 rifles per month totaling 852,088 Mosin-Nagant rifles. Concurrently, the plant manufactured 10,000 Russian and British bayonets per day.

In February 2017, a gravely ill Czar Nicholas II abdicated his throne. The Russian Revolution that followed was, in actuality, a series of two revolutions. The first one overthrew the Imperial government, and the second established the Bolsheviks in power. The incoming Communist government repudiated the contract, refusing to accept delivery of the arms and ammunition or to pay for the them. Their excuse was specious, claiming the weapons were of poor quality. In truth, Remington and NEWs were superior to the Russian-made rifles. So as it came to pass, arms merchants New England Westinghouse and Remington were stuck with hundreds of thousands of Mosin-Nagants.

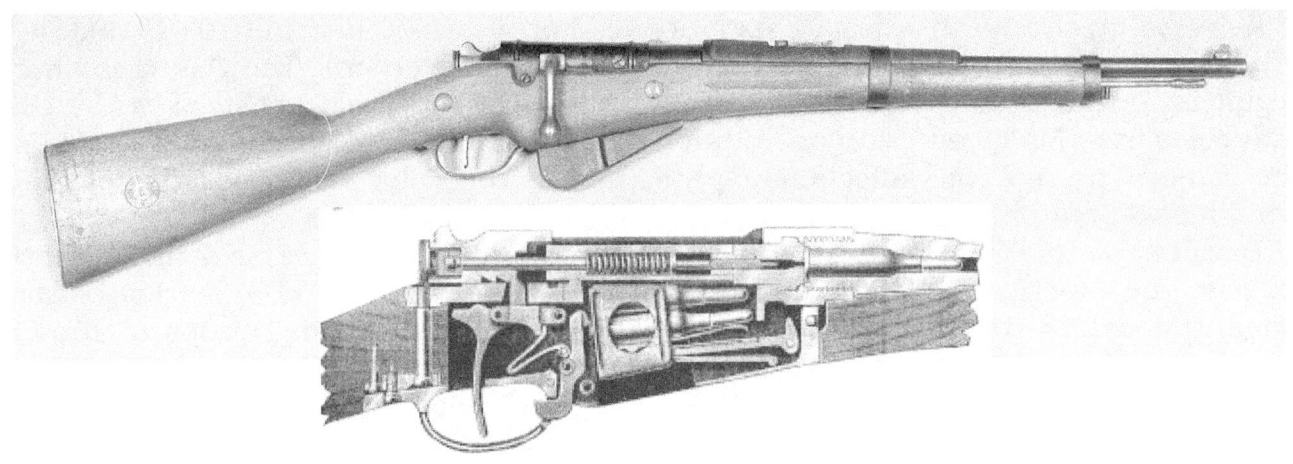

Berthier Model 1916 Carbine, by Swedish Army Museum, *Licensed under 4.0 International (CC BY 4.0)*

The massive default would have caused many companies to stagger and go broke. Remington almost did. New England Westinghouse, though shifted gears securing a U.S. Government contract to build Browning M1918 rifles at its Stevens-Duryea plant.

Ultimately the U.S. government bought the undelivered rifles, saving Remington and Westinghouse from bankruptcy. Many undelivered rifles sold as military surplus and on the black market. Some surplus rifles were re-chambered in the American 30-'06 cartridge.

Westinghouse Co. archives claim surplus weapons were sold to the British to supplement their Lee-Enfields in the trenches. Military arms glutted the world market by war's end, and manufacturers unloaded surplus into the black market, frequently selling to the highest bidder. The U.S. Congress launched many inquiries into wartime profiteering and an investigation of those companies with close ties to the fallen tzarist government.

U.S. Rifle, 7.62 mm Model of 1916 In Military Hands

The rifles in Great Britain armed the U.S. and British expeditionary forces sent to North Russia in 1918 and 1919. Rifles still in the U.S. ended up being training firearms for the U.S. Army. Some equipped the U.S. National Guard, SATC, and ROTC. Designated as the U.S. Rifle, 7.62mm, Model of 1916", these are among the most obscure U.S. service arms In 1917, 50,000 rifles were shipped via Vladivostok to equip Czechoslovak Legions stranded in Siberia to aid in securing passage to France.

The Mosin-Nagant's Model 1891's wartime service with U.S. troops was not limited to stateside duty. When Bolsheviks seized power in 1917, the Allies had already shipped considerable military aid to the Czar. The powers that be concluded that the war material should not fall into the hands of the revolutionaries.

As a result, the North Russia Expeditionary Force formed in June 1918. Made up of young draftees, the 339th Infantry got its marching orders. The 339th infantry regiment affectionately referred to as Detroit's Own derived most of its 4,487 inductees from Michigan. With an additional 500 draftees from Wisconsin included in the ranks. The unit was affectionately nicknamed the Polar Bears because of their pending destination of Siberia.

Because of the large quantities of 7.62x54r ammunition stockpiled in Northern Russia, the American soldiers traded 03 Springfields and M1917 rifles for Mosin-Nagant Model 1891s, which eased the logistical woes of deploying troops to such a far-flung location as Archangel. American soldiers were not fond of the M91s. They disliked the bayonet. They considered the sights hopelessly crude compared to the 1903 Springfield. That said, the M91s performed well enough in combat.

American troops deployed along a 450-mile long front, from Onega in the west to Pinega in the east. And at points 200 miles distant from the Archangel base. Elements of the 339th Infantry covered the main avenues of approach to Archangel from the south. Between September 1918 and May 1919, operations against the Soviet forces resulted in more than 500 American casualties.

During the interwar period, the rifles taken over by the U.S. military were sold by the Director of Civilian Marksmanship to private citizens in the United States by the predecessor agency to the current Civilian Marksmanship Program. They sold for the princely sum of $3.00 each. Unaltered to chamber U.S..30-06 Springfield rimless, these rifles are prized by collectors for their absence of import marks required by law to be stamped or engraved on military surplus firearms imported to the United States.

As mentioned early on, during the early days of World War I, Russia was unable to build as many Mosin Nagant rifles as its army needed. So, in 1915, the Tsar's emissary ordered a million and a half M1891 Mosin-Nagants from Remington, replete with matching bayonets, and another one million and eight hundred thousand rifles from New England Westinghouse. Remington's largest single order for military rifles during World War I called for the delivery of one million 7.62x52R Mosin-Nagant Military Rifles replete with bayonets at the cost of $30 each. These Remington-made Mosin Nagants were nearly identical to their Russian-made counterparts. On July 16, 1915, The Russian Government gave Remington another order for an additional 200,000 rifles and a final order on September 15, 1915, for 300,000 more rifles. The total of all three contracts: 1,500,000 rifles.

By November 15, 1917, some 513,138 Mosin-Nagant rifles were accepted for delivery to Russia. Despite the low average cost, the M91/30 rifles were well-made, accurate, and flawlessly reliable. Aficionados are in agreement Remington-built Mosin-Nagants are of superior fit and finish compared to war-time Soviet production rifles.

In February 1917, Imperial Russia's Czar Nicholas II was overthrown. The Provisional Kerensky Government took over, halting the Remington/New England

Soldiers of Company A armed with U.S.-made M1891 Mosin-Nagants.

Westinghouse Mosin-Nagant contracts, with a little more than half of the original contract rifles having been delivered in exile to use American credits to purchase additional rifles to supply anti- Bolshevik forces fighting back in Mother Russia. Facing the prospect of a horrific economic loss after Russia defaulted on its weapon's debt, Remington was relieved when the U.S. Government purchased most of the remaining completed rifles, about 78,950 of them. Production resumed under an agreement between the Imperial Russian Embassy and the United States government for a time.

Re-Purposed Mosin M1916s

When in 1917, the United States joined Britain and France in World War One, it lacked sufficient numbers of rifles to arm the American Expeditionary Force that was soon to deploy to Europe's Western Front. In addition to needing rifles for troops in combat, weapons were also necessary for stateside training: Teaching troops how to march, how to perform close order drill, to pull guard duty, and the like. Serendipitously, both Remington UMC and New England Westinghouse were stuck with a boatload of Mosin-Nagant rifles the Bolsheviks did not want to pay for.

Disaster loomed. That is at least until the U.S. government purchased the Russian rifles. Doing so not only prevented financial ruin, it freed up 1903 Springfields and Model 1917s for shipment to the Western Front. Mosin-Nagant rifles of military design durable were designated Russian Three-line Rifle, Caliber 7.62 mm (.3 inch), and inducted into the U.S. Army. Those purchased rifles have Russian inspectors stamps and were stamped in the stock with a US stamp and an Ordnance bomb in the wood in front of the trigger guard to signify US ownership

American troops parade down the street in Vladivostok. - Siberia, August 1918

The Armistice for the war to end all wars, went into effect at 11:00 am on the 11th of

November 1918, marking the end of combat on the western front. While armistice day came and went, there was no change for the American soldiers fighting in Siberia. They were not withdrawn from combat and shipped stateside until well into 1919 Ironically, despite the intended purpose of the North Russia campaign, American troops abandoned their rifles to the Bolsheviks rather than bring them home.

The U.S. Army brass had contempt for the Mosin-Nagants and got rid of them when and wherever possible. One example, in November 1918, seventy-seven thousand rifles were given to the then-fledgling country of Czechoslovakia. Shipped from Remington's Connecticut factory to Vladivostok by way of Vancouver, Canada.

Bolshevik POWs being fed by an American soldier with a Mosin Nagant rifle by his side. Archangel 1918.

After World War I, five-thousand American-made Model 1891 rifles ended up in Mexico in an arms deal with the United States. With all its internal problems due to their revolution's constant fighting, Mexico was in desperate need of guns. Some Remington and Westinghouse rifles ended up in Finland and some in Spain due to the civil wars fought within those countries.

Firearms from Finland typically featured the letters-SA prominently roll-stamped on the receiver. Spanish guns with their replacement stocks show the letters MP stamped over the number 8. Some American-made Mosin-Nagants were rumored to have come from Mexico wrapped in Mexican newspapers, this according to men of the XV International Brigade, alternatively known as the Abraham Lincoln Brigade. These American-made M1891s were dubbed Mexicanskis.

Many more American-made Mosins were sold off to surplus companies, most notably by Francis Bannerman & Sons. Bannerman's converted a great many to caliber .30-06 and sporterized them, turning them into hunting rifles. Some were kept as is and sold as surplus.

The US then contracted with Westinghouse to continue manufacturing the rifles as the government was having Westinghouse manufacture the Browning Machine guns. Still, the contract wasn't finalized yet, and they didn't want to lose the experienced workforce at Westinghouse. During this contract, an additional 200 thousand rifles were manufactured. These final rifles were thoroughly inspected by US inspectors and have US inspection stamps and Ordnance bombs on the barrel, bolt, and receiver. They are considered a legitimate US firearm.

Interesting to note, some aficionados believe that designated Model 1916 contract rifles that didn't get delivered to Russia were a newly-made rifle under a separate US contract, not a Russian, and it have only US inspectors stamps on it are a legitimate US firearm and are a different variant than the ones left undelivered

Some aficionados believe the Westinghouse rifles for the Russians were manufactured in the US with British owned machinery and the Russia contracts were actually via the British Government who funded much of the project in attempt to keep Russia supplied with weapons to help keep it in the war. This rifle is part of the extra 200,00 that was produced under the US government contract with no attachment to the Russia or British contracts.

Civilian Use

Since 1960, as Finland's military modernized, it exported Mosin-Nagants in goody numbers. Most ended up as inexpensive surplus for Western nations. In Russia, the Mosin-Nagant action was the foundation for many commercial rifles. The most famous Vostok target rifles exported to Europe in the 1960s and 1970s were chambered in the standard 7.62×54mmRR round and also 6.5×54mmR, a necked-down version of the original cartridge designed for long-range target shooting. Rifles in 6.5×54mmR chambering necked-down 7.62×54mmR cartridges were the USSR's Olympic biathlon team standard rifle until the International Olympic Committee revised rules reduced the range to 50 meters and required competitors to shoot rifles chambered in .22 Long Rifle.

Between the two World Wars, through the Director of Civilian Marksmanship Program, the U.S. government sold a number of the New England Westinghouse and Remington Model 1891s to private citizens in the United States. Today those rifles are valuable collectibles. Re-chambered by wholesalers, many American-made Mosin-Nagants were converted to the ubiquitous American .30-06 Springfield cartridge. Some crudely converted, others professionally. Suffice it to say, regardless of conversion quality. A qualified gunsmith ought to examine the rifle. Owners should take caution before firing commercial ammunition. Russian Springfield sold by Bannermann back in the day for $14 are M1891 Mosin-Nagants with the 7.62x54R chamber reamed longer to accommodate the greater overall length of the .30-06 Springfield cartridge case. Not a good idea: The rear of the 7.62x54R chamber measures .02 thousands of an inch wider in diameter than the .30-06 Springfield case. That dimension invites case-rupture on firing. Be advised M1891 actions handle escaping gas poorly.

When the Iron Curtain collapsed in 1990, many Mosin-Nagants found their way into markets as collectibles and hunting rifles. Due to the large surplus from World War II and the propensity of the former Soviet Union to hoard large quantities of surplus, M1891/30 rifles, and M1944 carbines are inexpensively priced compared to competing surplus weapons.

Sailors from the USS Olympic, armed with US Rifle 7.62 Model of 1916 rifles. Notice how the sailor on the bottom left is holding a hand grenade.

These days, among collectors, there is significant interest in the Mosin-Nagant family of rifles. With a deserved reputation for durability and reliability, they are popular with target shooters and hunters. However, one undeniable weak point shooting is the coarse Soviet military sights. The notched rear tangent iron sight calibrated in hundreds of meters (Arshins on earlier models) adjusts for elevation. The front sight post does not adjust for elevation. The armory adjusts windage before issue. Drifting a dovetail mount allows for corrections in the field.

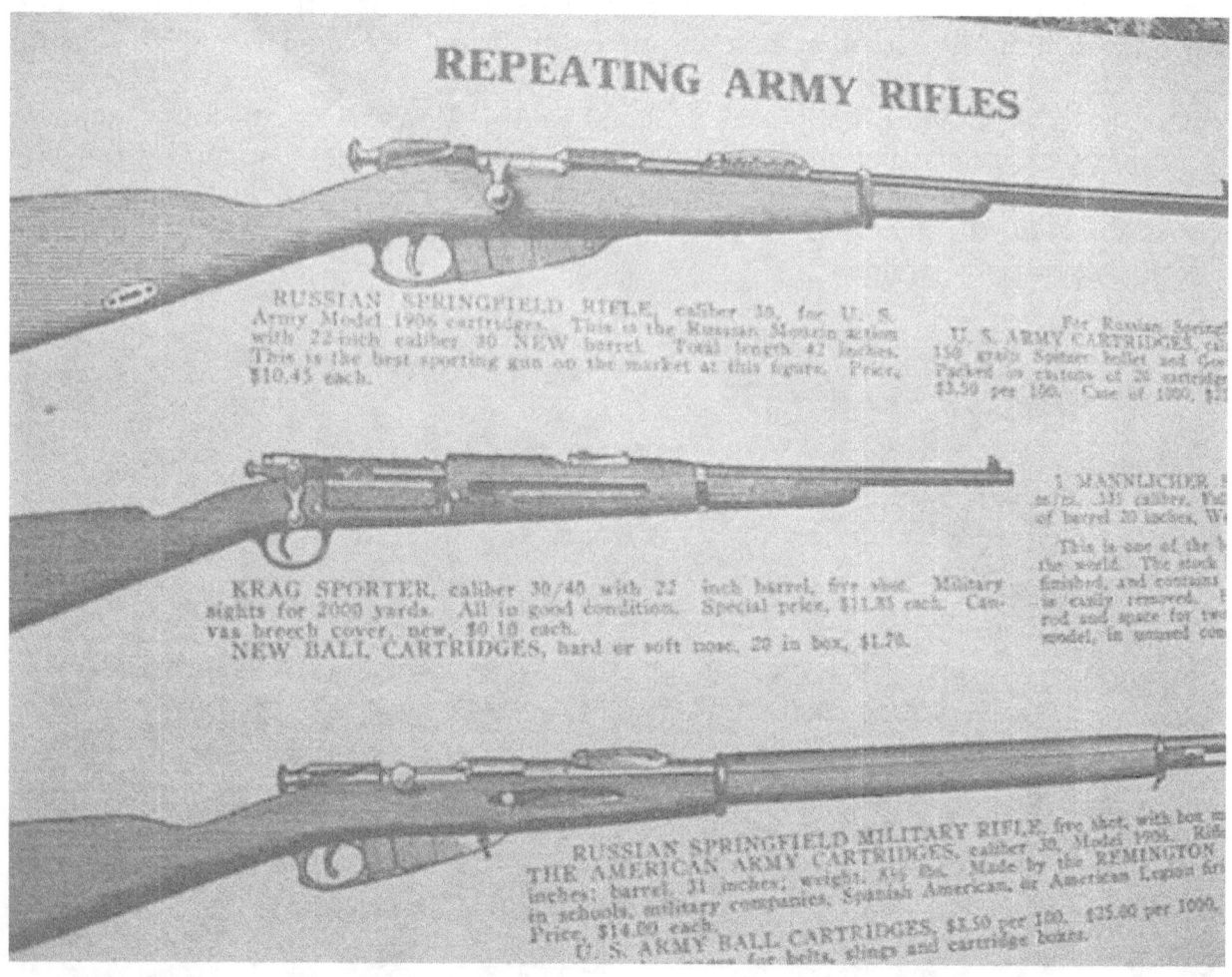

Billed as The Russian Springfield Rifle, chambered in .30-'06, Westinghouse and Remington built Mosin-Nagants sold alongside sporterized 30-40 Krags.

40.8-mm Dyakanov Rifle Grenade Launcher

The 40.8-mm Dyakonov Rifle Grenade Launcher (ружейный гранатомёт Дьяконова), designed in 1916 by its namesake, Capt. Mikhail Dyakonov passed military trials, but due to the Russian revolution a year later, it was not put into service until 1928. Albeit in a slightly improved version with better sights and longer effective range. The design was not new, derived from a device issued in small numbers during World War One.

A single Dyakonov was issued per rifle squad until 1938 when the Red Army reorganized its divisional structure, and the Dyakonov launchers were separated from the individual squads. A platoon-level grenade section was created, with a battery of 3 launchers.

Dyakonov used a standard M91/30 rifle. Its kit includes the grenade cup, tripod, sight, and a piece to fit over the buttstock to be driven into the ground when firing. It was not meant to be fired from the shoulder because it would break the soldier's collarbone. Two unique bags were issued to grenadiers to carry gear and ammunition.

Similar to a bayonet, the Dyakonov launcher cup fits over the muzzle of the M91/30. Furthermore, the launcher's rifled barrel attaches to the muzzle of a standard Mosin Nagant M1891/30 rifle secured by the bayonet lugs. A tripod and sighting device connects to the gun. Grenades are fired with standard cartridges, no blank round is needed. The bullet triggers the launching charge to an effective range of 150-850 meters, depending on charge and ammo used. Its two main rounds are flare and fragmentation. The standard HE round weighs 340g/7.5 pounds, measuring 40mm in diameter. In April 1941, the Dyakonov was replaced at the rifle platoon level by a 50mm mortar.

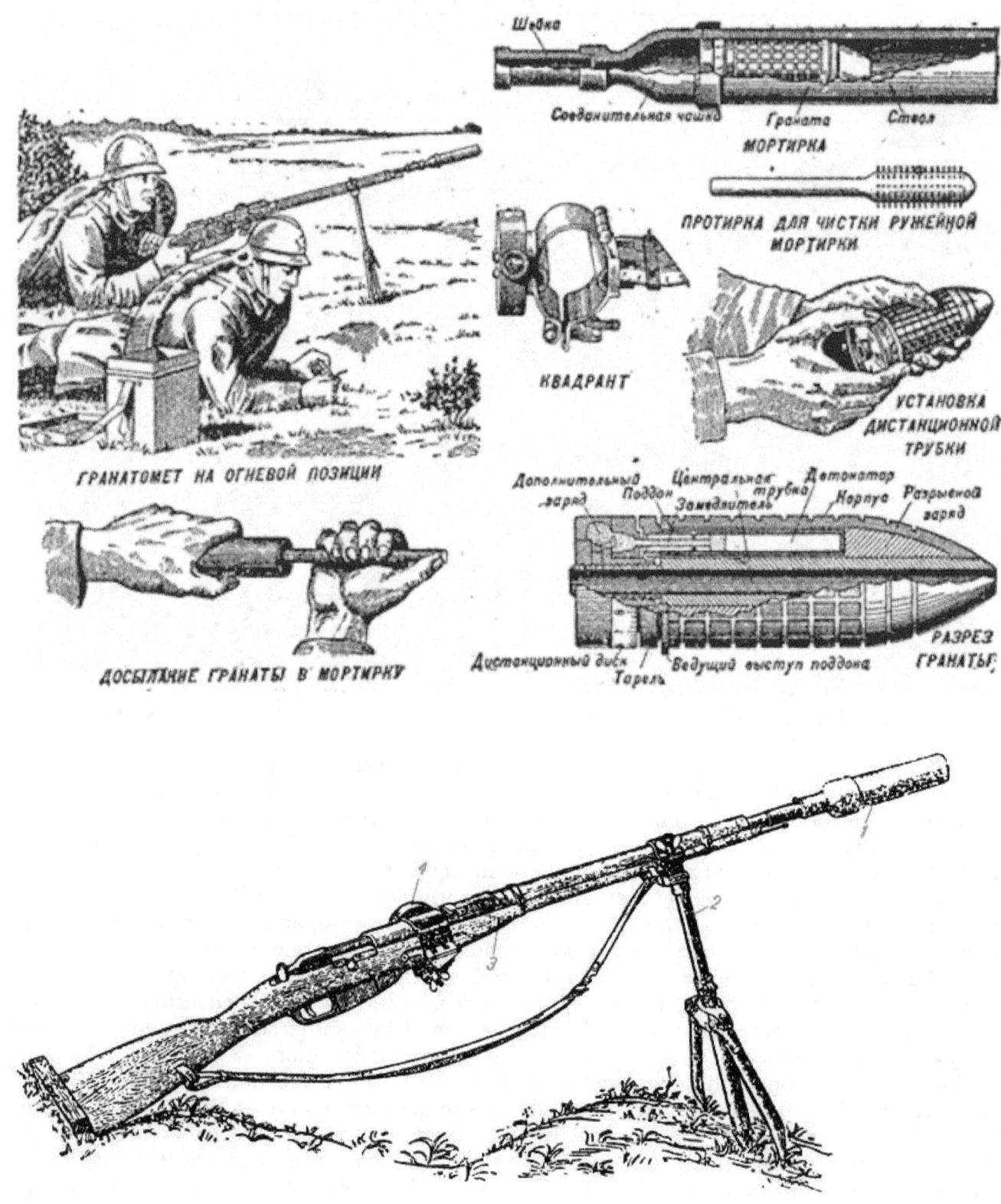

Mosin-Nagant Accessories

A soldier field strips his weapon.

Each Mosin-Nagant rifle and carbine is provided with a one-piece cleaning rod which is fitted in the stock. The rod is threaded to take the tapped receiver nut embedded in the stock just below the chamber. An accessory pouch carried by each rifleman contains a screwdriver, oil can, clean rod head, cleaning rod brush, cleaning rod attachment, rod collar, and cleaning rod stop. There are variations in the design of the oil can and screwdriver.

Accessories for the Mosin-Nagant: Bottles for bore solvent/lubricant; Broken case extractor; Screwdriver, also used to set striker depth. Photo courtesy LibertyTreeCollectors.com

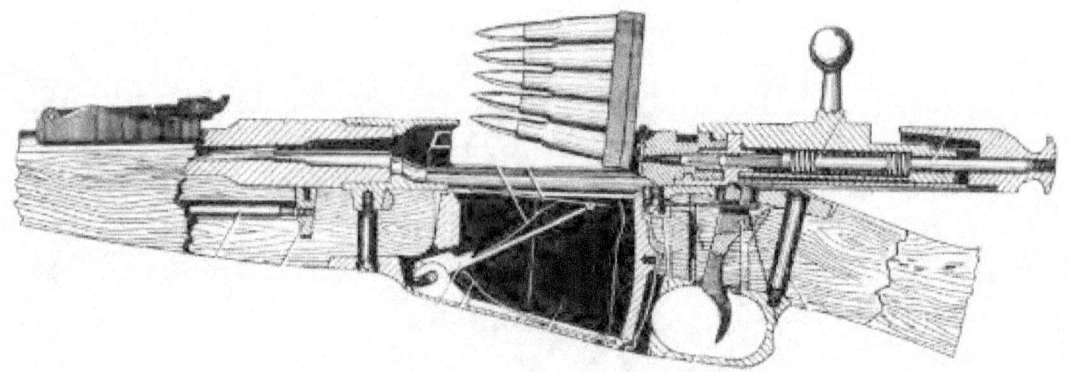

POSITION OF PARTS PRIOR TO LOADING THE RIFLE.

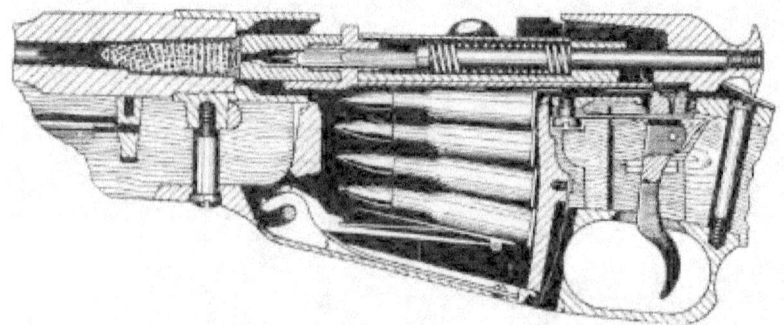

POSITION OF PARTS AFTER RIFLE IS LOADED.

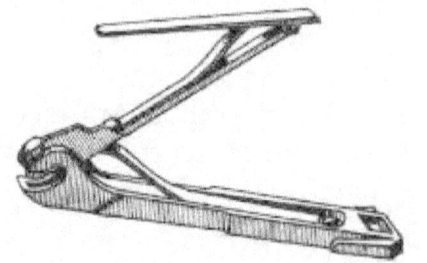

FOLLOWER AND FLOOR PLATE.

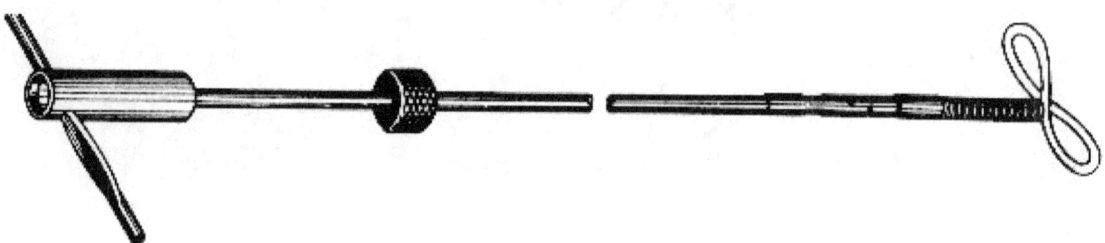

An assembled cleaning rod handle, muzzle protector and jag.

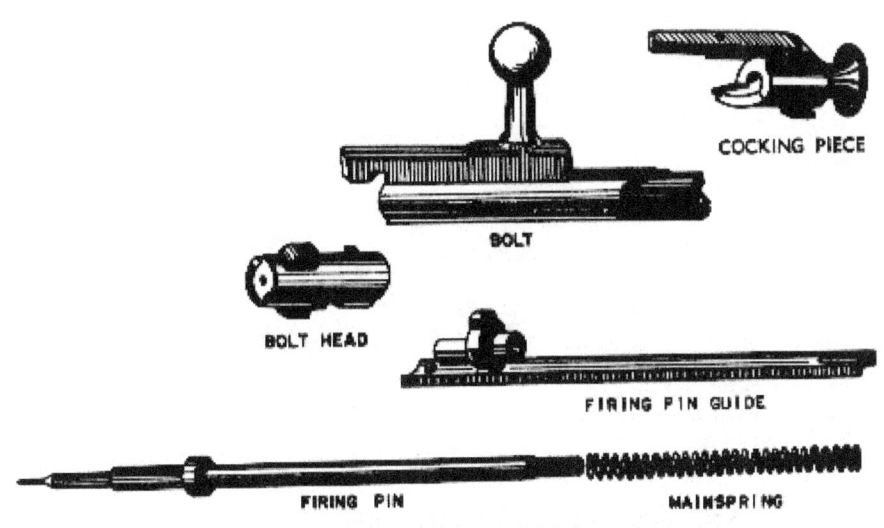
BOLT ASSEMBLY COMPONENTS.

Field Stripping the Mosin-Nagant

Unbuckle the dog collars and remove the sling from the slots. Unscrew the cleaning rod by rotating it counterclockwise. Depressing the barrel band retaining springs, slide the barrel bands forward past the end of the stock. Remove the handguard. On some models, the front sight will block the barrel band removal.

Decock the bolt by turning the cocking knob 90-degrees counterclockwise and pulling the bolt head and connector bar forward. Rotate the bolt head 90 degrees clockwise and pull it off the connector bar. Use the large notch on the bolt tool or the connector bar as a wrench, grasp the firing pin between the fingers and unscrew it counterclockwise. Caution: Grasp it firmly as the spring is under pressure.

Turn the cocking knob 90 degrees counterclockwise to decock the bolt. Pulling the bolt head and connector bar forward. Rotate the bolt head 90 degrees clockwise. Use either the large notch on the bolt tool or the connector bar as a wrench to pull it off the connector bar. Grasp the firing pin and unscrew it counterclockwise. Caution: Grasp it firmly as the spring is under pressure.

Remove both the magazine assembly and receiver assemblies from the stock. Some Russian and Soviet Mosin Nagants, especially Finnish, feature shims at the tang and recoil lugs. Noting their location, take care not to lose the shims. The trigger pin, held in place only by the stock, can fall out when removed,

Depress the magazine floorplate latch. Pull the floorplate away from the magazine body. Compressing the follower assembly, pull it straight down and out of the magazine body.

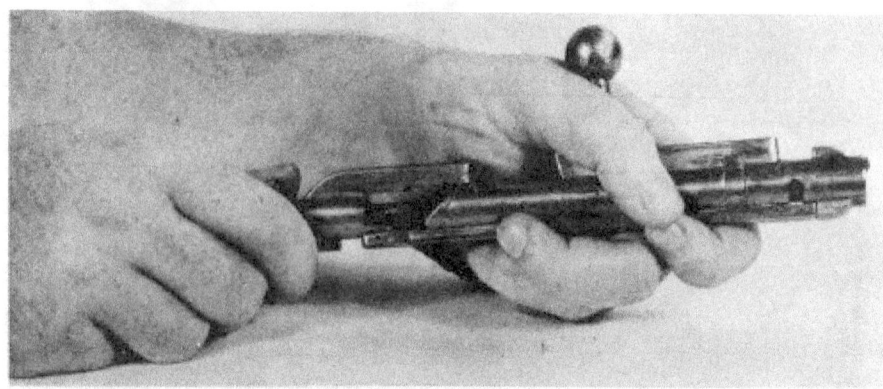

To disassemble the bolt, draw the cocking piece back and rotate it to the left to relieve spring pressure.

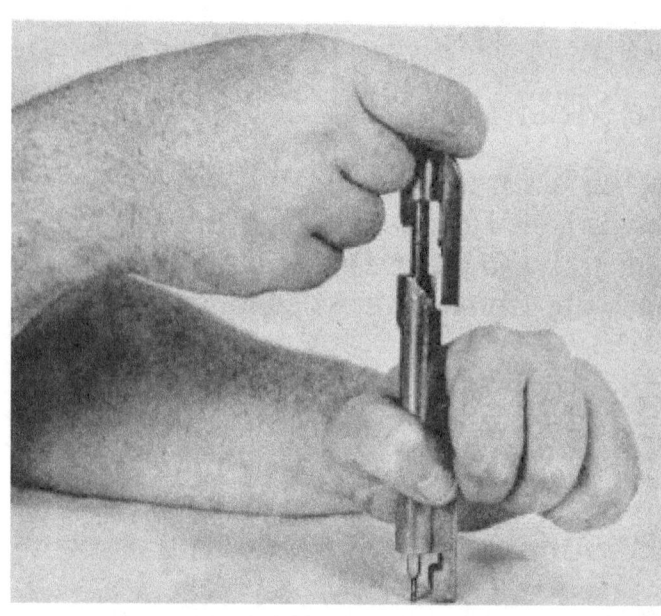

Place the firing pin on a solid surface, push the bolt body down, unscrew the cocking piece, and then remove the firing pin and spring. When re-assembling, make sure the butt of the firing pin is flush with the cocking piece and that the marks on the firing pin align with those on the cocking piece to assure correct firing pin protrusion.

Remove the Mosin-Nagant barreled action from the stock by taking off the two barrel bands by depressing the spring keepers that hold the bands to the rifle. Next, lift off the handguards, invert the rifle and remove the action bolts at either end. The barreled action will now lift out of the stock, and the bottom metal consisting of the entire magazine trigger guard assembly can be removed. Reverse assembly is the reverse procedure. The screwdriver provided in the accessory kit can be used for this purpose.

Stock bands are removed by turning the screw to the right to expand the bands, then slipping the bands forward and off the stock. To remove the one-piece interrupter-ejector, remove the screw and push the interrupter-ejector forward until it is disengaged from the dovetail.

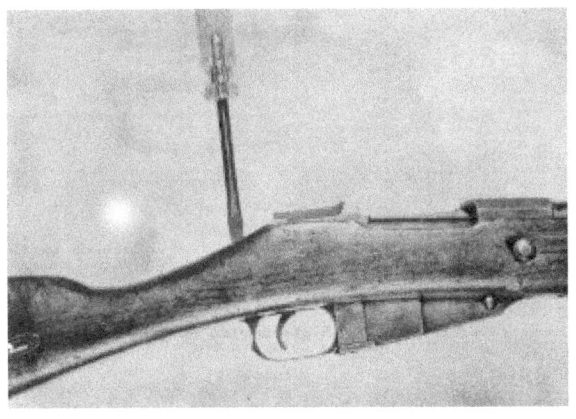 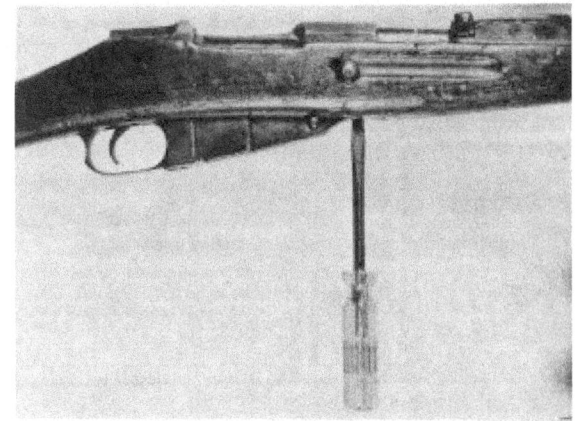

Remove both action bolts.

MAGAZINE AND TRIGGER GUARD.

How to Disassemble the Magazine Floorplate

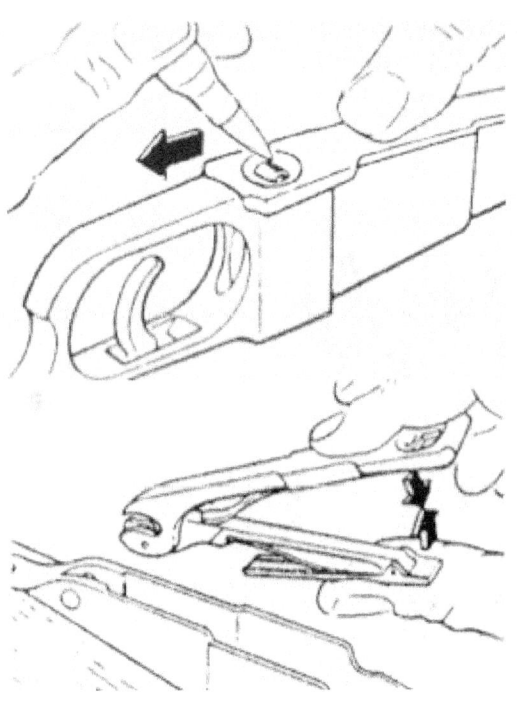

Disassemble the magazine floorplate and follower assembly by push back the floorplate release button with a finger, bullet tip, or similar implement and swinging the hinged floorplate open. Next, squeeze the floorplate and follower together, thereby opening the floorplate hinge allowing it to pull free of the magazine housing.

The 7.62 X 54R Cartridge

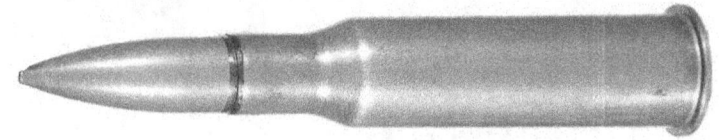

Muzzle velocity - Light ball	865 m/s (2,838 ft/s) rifle 800 m/s (2,625 ft/s) carbine.
Effective firing range	500 m (550 yards), 800+ m (875+ yards with optics)
Feed system	5-round non-detachable magazine, loaded individually or with 5-round stripper clips
Sights	**M91/30** **Rear:** ladder, graduated from 100 m to 2,000 m and from 100 m to 1,000 m **M38 and M44** **Front:** hooded fixed post (drift adjustable) PU 3.5 and PEM scope also mounted.

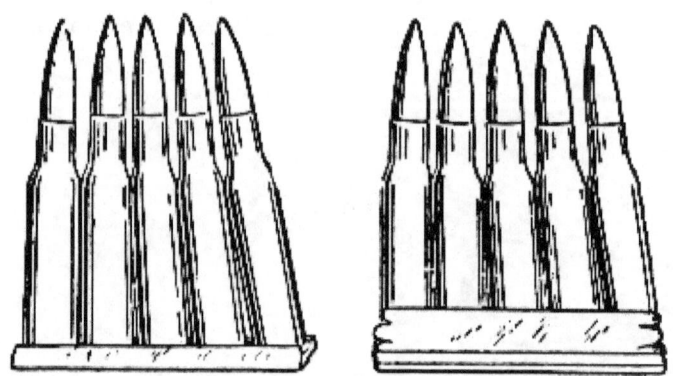

FIGURE 34. SOVIET FIVE-ROUND CARTRIDGE CLIPS.

The Lineage of the 7.62 X 54mm R Cartridge

First issued in 1891 to the Imperial Russian Army, the 7.62x54R caliber was the first smokeless powder cartridge. It also qualifies as the longest-running issued cartridge globally, drawing combat pay with SVD rifles and PKM machine guns. During its many years of service, the bullet weight and powder charge have evolved. In its original incarnation, the load was a 212-grain round-nose bullet with a muzzle velocity of 2020 feet per second. In 1908, it transitioned to a 147-grain spitzer bullet traveling downrange at about 2800 fps.

In 1966, to enhance accuracy, for the Dragunov SVD, the Soviets developed the 7N1 variant, developed by V. M. Sabelnikov, P. P. Sazonov, and V. M. Dvorianinov. It loaded match-grade extruded powder instead of coarser ball propellant. It had a 9.8 g (151.2 gr) boat-tailed FMJ jacketed projectile replete with an air pocket, steel core, and a lead knocker in its base for the maximum terminal effect. It had a ballistic coefficient (G1 BC) of approximately 0.411 and (G7 BC) of about 0.206.

package of 20 sniper rounds 7N14

Produced by Factory 188, the Novosibirsk Low Voltage Equipment Plant, cartridges are head-stamped with the number 188 and the year of manufacture. Rounds are packaged 20 per paper packet, with 22 packets to a metal spam-can tin. There are two 440-round tins per wooden case for a total of 880 rounds. The individual paper packets, hermetically sealed metal spam cans, and wooden shipping crates are distinctly marked *Снайперская* (*Snaiperskaya*) for sniper. The wax wrapping paper for the paper packets is covered in red text to avoid misusing it. As hard body armor saw its way onto battlefields, the 7N1 was replaced in 1999 by the 7N14 special load developed for the SVD.

The 7N14 round features a 9.8 gram/151.2 grain projectile with a sharp hardened steel core to improve penetration. Average muzzle velocity is 830 m/second 2,723 feet per second, for a muzzle energy of 3,375 J (2,489 ft·lb-feet).

7.62×53mmR (Finland) Versus 7.62×54mmR (Russia)

The Finnish 7.62 X 53mmR is virtually identical to the Russian 7.62 X 54mmR military cartridge Restated for emphasis, the Finnish 7.62×53mmR is a variant of the Russian 7.62×54mmR. The two cartridges are interchangeable.

However, in the older version, the Finnish military cartridge was loaded with the S-type bullet with its nominal diameter of .308. In 1936 the Finnish Army unveiled a new service cartridge intended for machine guns and rifles. Its new bullet, the D-16, nominal diameter measured .310. Coincidentally, the new M39 service rifle, with its nominal bore diameter of .310, had been designed around the D-166 cartridge.

Hand-loaded cartridges for Finnish rifles should use .308 inches (7.8 mm) diameter bullets with other Finnish Mosin-Nagant variants instead of the bigger 0.310 inches (7.9 mm), giving the best results in M39, Soviet, and most of the other Mosin-Nagant rifles.

Dimensional Differences Between 7.62 × 53 R & 7.62 × 54 R

	53R	54R
Length Overall	77.00 mm	77.16 mm
Case length	53.50 mm	53.72 mm
Rim diameter	14.40 mm	14.48 mm
Bullet diameter	7.85 mm	7.92 mm

Lapua, the Finnish commercial ammunition manufacturer, does not differentiate between the 53R and 54R, producing cartridges that function in weapons chambered for either caliber.

Barnaul, the Russian ammunition maker, states Russian cartridges marked 7.62×53 are virtually identical with 7.62×54. The letter-R indicates a case rim.

Novosibirsk Cartridge Plant L.V.E. another Russian ammunition manufacturer, states, "Producers mark these cartridges differently, leading to confusion based on differences in rounding up or rounding down cartridge case length. You may use cartridges of caliber 7.62x54R freely with arms marked 7.62×53R.

Deciphering a Spam Can

Cartridge Case Material	Composition
ГЖ	Bimetallic case (gilding metal clad steel)
ГЛ	Brass case
ГС	Steel case

Bullet Type	Composition
ЛПС	Light ball bullet with mild steel core
ПС-	Sniper round with mild steel core bullet

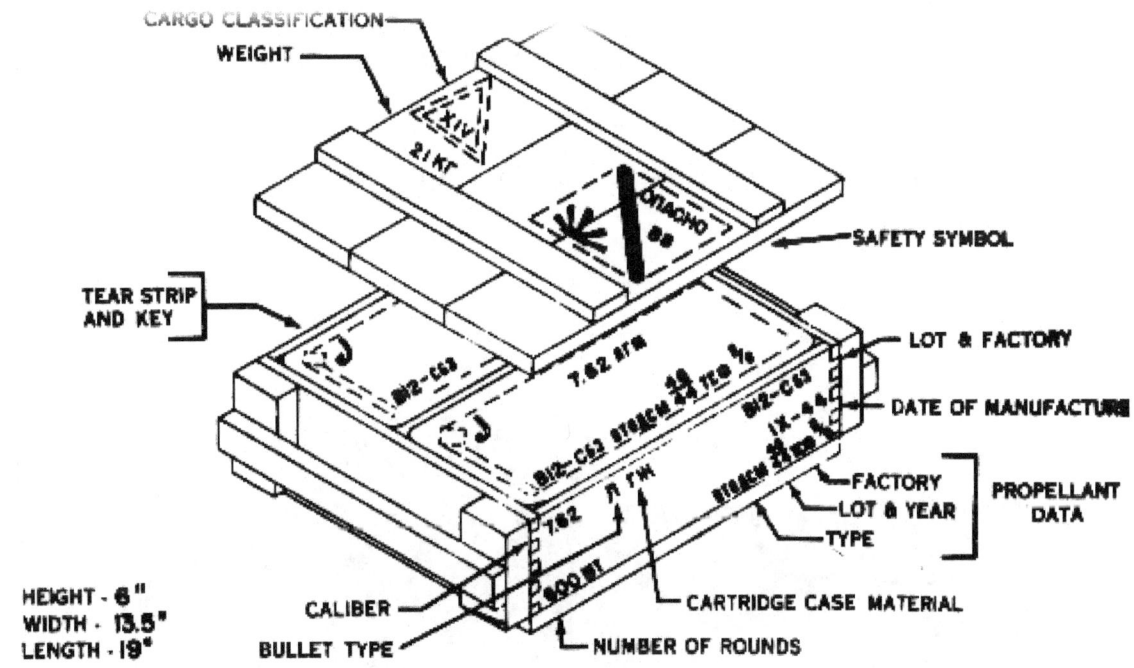

Basic Specifications 21st-Century Russian Military Loads

While there are several variants of Russian military 7.62×54mmR rounds intended for machine guns and sniper rifles, all bullet jackets and tracer cups are copper-washed steel and all variants use clad metal as case material.

57-N-323S	This conventional steel-core bullet is intended for engaging personnel and weapon systems. Its steel-core bullet and ballistic coefficient (G1 BC) is approximately 0.374 and (G7 BC) of about 0.187. The tip, sans distinguishing color, can penetrate a 6 mm (0.2 in) thick St3 steel plate at 520 m (569 yds) and 6Zh85T body armor at 110 m (120 yds).
7N13	This enhanced-penetration bullet's heat-strengthened core can kill personnel wearing body armor. The tip is uncolored. A sealing lacquer belt on the mouth of the case is red-colored. It can penetrate a 6 mm (0.2 in) thick St3 steel plate at 660 m (722 yds) and 6Zh85T body armor at 800 m (875 yds).
7T2	A variant of the T-46 tracer bullet, designed for fire adjustment and target designation, has a green tip. The green trace burns for 3 seconds.
7BZ3	A B-32 variant this armor-piercing/incendiary bullet penetrates lightly armored 'targets. The bullet tip is black-red
7N1	Designed for enhanceed accuracy the sniper round bullet tip is uncolored.

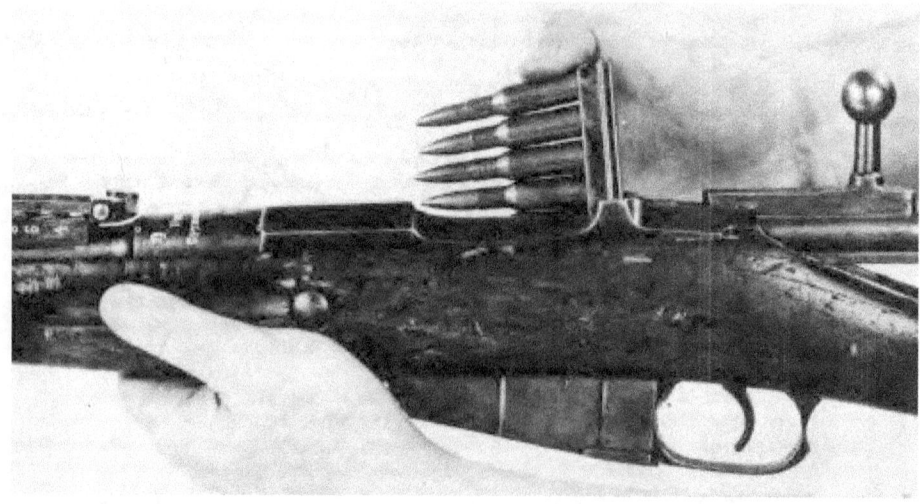

Clip loading a Mosin-Nagant

Cartridge Designations

Designation	57-N-323S	7N13 (AP)	7T2 (tracer)	7BZ3 (API)	7N1
Cartridge weight	21.8 g (336 gr)	21.7 g (335 gr)	22 g (340 gr)	22.6 g (349 gr)	21.9 g (338 gr)
Bullet weight	9.6 g (148.2 gr)	9.4 g (145.1 gr)	9.65 g (148.9 gr)	10.39 g (160.3 gr)	9.8 g (151.2 gr)
Muzzle velocity	828 m/s (2,717 ft/s)	828 m/s (2,717 ft/s)	798 m/s (2,618 ft/s)	809 m/s (2,654 ft/s)	823 m/s (2,700 ft/s)
Muzzle energy	3,291 J (2,427 ft·lbf)	3,222 J (2,376 ft·lbf)	3,073 J (2,267 ft·lbf)	3,400 J (2,508 ft·lbf)	3,319 J (2,448 ft·lbf)
Accuracy of fire at 300 m (328 yd)	90 mm (3.5 in) (R50)	90 mm (3.5 in) (R50)	150 mm (5.9 in) (R50)	150 mm (5.9 in) (R50)	80 mm (3.1 in) (R100)

R50 at 300 m (328 yards) indicates the closest 50% of a shot group will print within a circle of the mentioned diameter at 300 m (328 yards).

R100 at 300 m (328 yds) indicates every shot of a shot group will be print within a circle of the mentioned diameter at 300 m (328 yards).

Designation	Transliteration	Meaning		Color Code	Production Years
ЛЛ	L	Light ball (lead core)		none	1910-1954
ДД	D	Long range (heavy ball lead core)		yellow tip	1930-1953
ЛПС	LPS	Light ball steel core		silver tip/none	1953-1991
Б-30	B-30	Armor Piercing with 1930 bullet		black tip	1930-1941
Б-32	B-32	Armor Piercing (Incendiary) 1932 bullet		black over red tip	1932-1969
Б-32М	B-32M	Armor Piercing (Incendiary) modernized 1932 bullet		black over red tip	1955-current
БС-40	BS-40	Armor Piercing (Incendiary) 1940 bullet		black tip over red bullet	1940-1941
БТ	BT	Armor Piercing Tracer		purple tip	1932-1937
БТ-90	BT-90	Armor Piercing Tracer		green tip	1998-current
БЗТ	BZT	Armor Piercing Incendiary Tracer		purple over red tip	1935-1940
ЗБ-46	ZB-46	Armor Piercing Incendiary Tracer		purple over red tip	WWII
ПЗ	PZ	Incendiary	Different designations for the same bullet	red tip	1935-current
ЗП	ZP	Incendiary		red tip	1935-current
ЗЗ	Z	Incendiary		red tip	1935-current
Т-30	T-30	Tracer with 1930 bullet		green tip	1930-1938
Т-46	T-46	Tracer with factory #46 bullet		green	1938-1974
Т-46М	T-46M	Tracer with modernized factory #46 bullet		green tip	1974-1995
Т-46М1	T-46M1	Tracer w modernized factory #46 bullet		green tip	1995-current
СН ПС	SN PS	Sniper (early 7N1 mark)		none	1967-1999
ПС	PS	Sniper (late 7N1 mark)		none	1967-1999
СНБ	SNB	Sniper/Armor Piercing (7N14 mark)		none	1999-current
УЗ	UZ	"Increased Charge" proof load		black bullet	1970s-current
ВД	BD	"High Pressure" proof load		yellow bullet	1970s-current
УС	US	Reduced Velocity		green bullet	1939-1941
Ц	Ts	Match			1954-1992
УЧ	UCh	Training			1950s-current
ПП	PP	Penetrating		None, green case	1993-current
БП	BP	Armor Piercing		black tip	1999-current
СТ-М2	ST-M2	Light ball steel core		none	1988-current
Х	Kh	Blank		not applicable	1926-current

Identifying Crates, Tins, and Wrapping

Terms, Abbreviations and Symbols	
Term	Meaning
В обоймах	On stripper clips
без обойм	Without stripper clips
герм. укупорка	Hermetically sealed
гермоукупорка	Hermetically sealed
ШКАС	Denotes the ShKAS aircraft machine gun
Propeller symbol (ellipsis)	ShKAS aircraft machine gun
винтовочые	(Rifle(s)
снайперские	Sniper (rifles)
холостые	Blank
Усиленный заряд	Increased Charge
Высокое давление	High Pressure
целевые	Match grade
учебные	Training
поверочные	Verifying
образцовые	Model
шт	Quantity

A Word About ShKAS Ammo

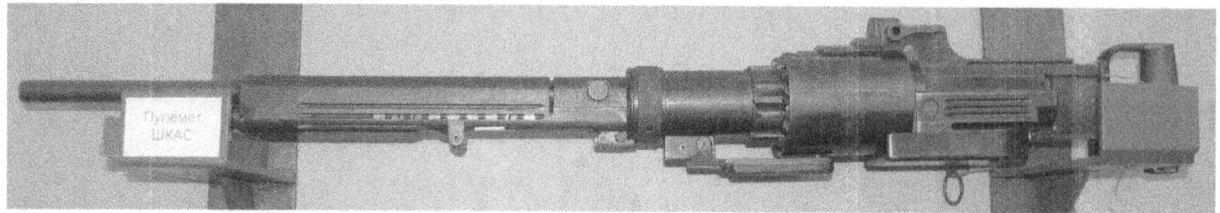

Soviet Russia's ShKAS (Shpitalny-Komaritsky Aircraft High-Speed Machine Gun) boasted an exceptionally high rate of fire. And while a high rate of fire tends to be a disadvantage in an infantry machine gun, in aircraft combat, it is imperative to have as many rounds down the barrel as possible. ShKAS boasted an eyebrow-raising 1800 rounds per minute with a single barrel! An updated version, the UltraShKAS, upped the rate of fire to an astounding 3000 rounds per minute. Fed from a disintegrating link metal belt, the ShKAS rate of fire put tremendous strain on cartridges. So special ammunition was loaded with thicker primers, cups and case heads, double crimped bullets, and a thicker case wall comprised of bimetallic construction instead of mere traditional brass. AP, API, APIT, explosive, and incendiary bullets were developed for the ShKAS ammunition to increase lethality. All ShKAS tolerances were tighter, including the powder charge.

Cartridges from the ShKAS production lines (including explosive and API rounds), which failed to meet QC standards, but were still functional, were issued to snipers and infantry units. Due to their to more precise powder charges, they were exceptionally accurate. Some aficionados incorrectly claim these rounds are of higher pressure than standard ammo and therefore unsafe for rifles. But this is false information. Restated for emphasis: ShKAS rounds do not have higher gas pressure! The difference, compared to rifle ammo: Thicker case walls on the sides to better withstand higher feeding stress). A deeper-seated, crimped primer. Early loads featured a double crimp on the case neck and a deeper-seated projectile. Because no API was specifically loaded for ground troops, ShKAS rounds were issued to the infantry during the Great Patriotic War with lacquered cases to ease extraction. To distinguish ShKAS from regular 7.62 ammunition, the case head was stamped with the letter Sh (Cyrillic -Ш).

Primary projectile	Armor-Piercing Incendiary B-32 bullet
Bullet weight	148 grains (9.6 grams)
Cartridge weight	370 grains (24 grams)
Ballistic coefficient	3.0 lb/in² (2,100 kg/m²)
Tracer illumination duration	750 m (2,460 ft)
Armor piercing penetration	11 mm (0.43 in) at 400 m (1,312 ft)

There were three different classes of Shaka cartridges, each one denominated by a different color code on the primer annulus.

- The 1st class ShKAS cartridge primer annulus was lacquered red, for use in synchronized ShKAS machine guns shooting between the propeller blades of single engine fighter planes.
- The 2nd class cartridges annulus was colorless, and was allowed in the observer's machine guns, or the ShKAS guns mounted to the wings of Ilyushin I-16 fighters or the nose of twin-engine bombers.
- 3rd class cartridges, with their black annulus, were wholly prohibited in ShKAS machine guns and were issued to the infantry. Which gives rise to the salient question. Exactly why were these rounds rejected from both 1st and second class? And did their shortcomings mean a drop off in accuracy or reliability?

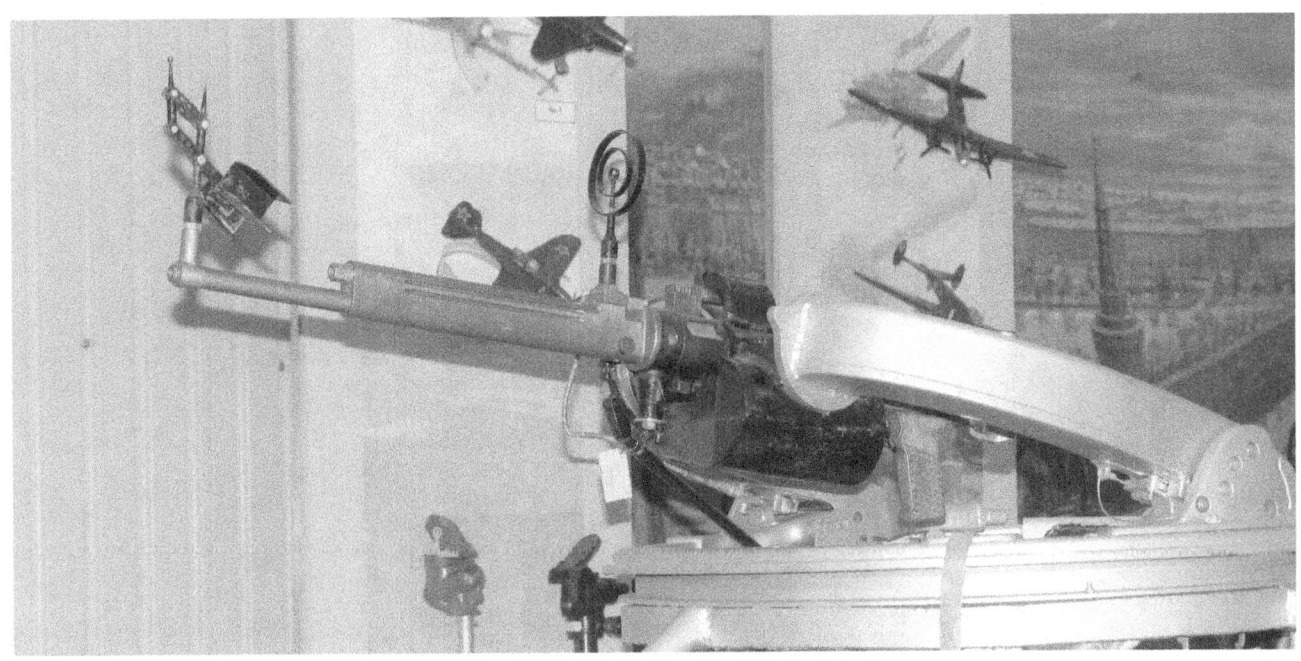

A ShKAS gun mounted in an observer's turret.

Cyrill. abbreviation	Russian meaning	English meaning
Б	broneboinij	armor piercing
БС	broneboinij spetsialnim	AP special (tungsten carbide core)
БК	broneboinij kumulyativnij	high explosive anti tank (HEAT)
БП	broneboinij prozhigaushij	high explosive anti tank (HEAT)
БР	broneboinij	armor piercing
БТ	broneboinij trasseruyushchey	armor piercing tracer
БЗ	broneboinij zazhigatelnij	armor piercing incendiary
БЗТ	broneboinij zazhigatelnij trasseruyushchey	armor piercing incendiary tracer
Д	dymovoj	smoke shell
ДРП	dynamo reaktivnaja pushka	recoilless cannon
Ф	fugasnij	high explosive
ФАБ	fugasnaja aviabomba	high explosive aircraft bomb
Г	god	year
ГЛ	gilza latun	brass cartridge case
ГЖ	gilza zheleznaya	gilding metal clad steel case
ГС	gilza stal	steel cartridge case
Х	cholostoy	blank cartridge
ХОЛ	cholostoy	blank cartridge, also on inert drill rounds and inert dummy fuzes
ИНЕРТ.	inertnuii	inert ordnance
ИНЕРТНЫЙ	inertnuii	inert ordnance
КА	Krasnaya Armiya	Red Army
Л	legkoy	light
ЛПС	legkoy puley stal	light ball with mild steel core
МАКЕТ	maket	inert ordnance
М	modernisirovanij	modernized
ОБР	obrazets	model
ОХ	?	inert ordnance
ОХО	?	inert ordnance
О	oskolochnij	fragmentation
ОФ	oskolochno-fugasnij	high explosive fragmentation
ОКБ	Opytno-Konstruktorskoe Buro	Pilot Design Bureau
ОТБ	Osoboe Tekhnicheskoe Buro	Special Technical Bureau
П	puley	bullet
П	podkalibernij	subcaliber (arrowhead shell)
ПС	puley stal	ball bullet with mild steel core
ПТ	puley trasseruyushchey	tracer bullet
ПЗ	puley zazhigatelnij	incentiary bullet
С	osvetitelnij	illumination shell
СП	sploshnoj	solid AP shell
Ш	shrapnel	canister shot shell
ШТ	shtuka	unit, pieces (number of rounds in box)
Ш	ShKAS	ammo for 7.62mm ShKAS aircraft MG
Т	trasseruyushchey	tracer
У	unitarnij	fixed ammunition
В	vystrel	separate loading ammo
З	zazhigatelnij	incendiary
ЗП	zazhigatelnij puley	incendiary bullet

Zeroing a howitzer with a Mosin-Nagant

The Fighting Weapons of Seven Warring Powers.

The German Mauser rate of fire is faster than any other rifle used in the war. Its magazine holds five cartridges, packed in chargers.

The Austrian Mannlicher is the lightest of all, yet its 244 grain bullet, is the heaviest used by any of the powers. It is very rapid in action.

The British short Lee-Enfield is the outcome of the South African War. It holds ten cartridges and is sighted from 200 to 2,800 yards.

The French Lebel is the longest rifle. The tube magazine under the barrel holds eight cartridges. The bullet weighs 198 grains.

The Belgian Mauser of 1889 holds five cartridges carried in clips. It cannot be used as a single loader. It weighs over eight pounds.

The Russian r3 Line ifle , 7 in. longer than the British, is capable of firing 24 bullets to the minute. The bayonet is always fixed.

The Italian Mannlicher-Carcano Modelo 1891 is slow, discharging a mere fifteen rounds per minute

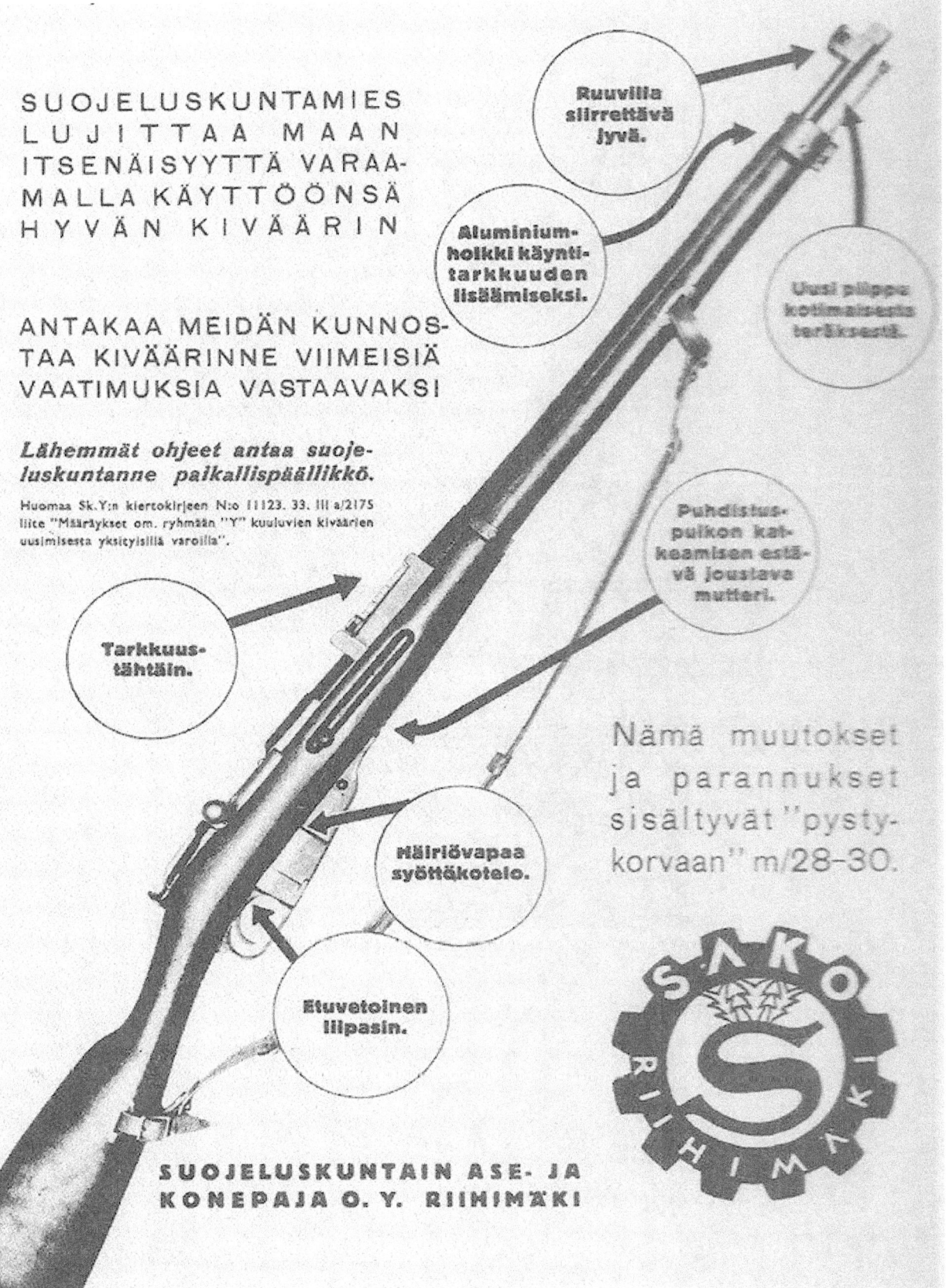

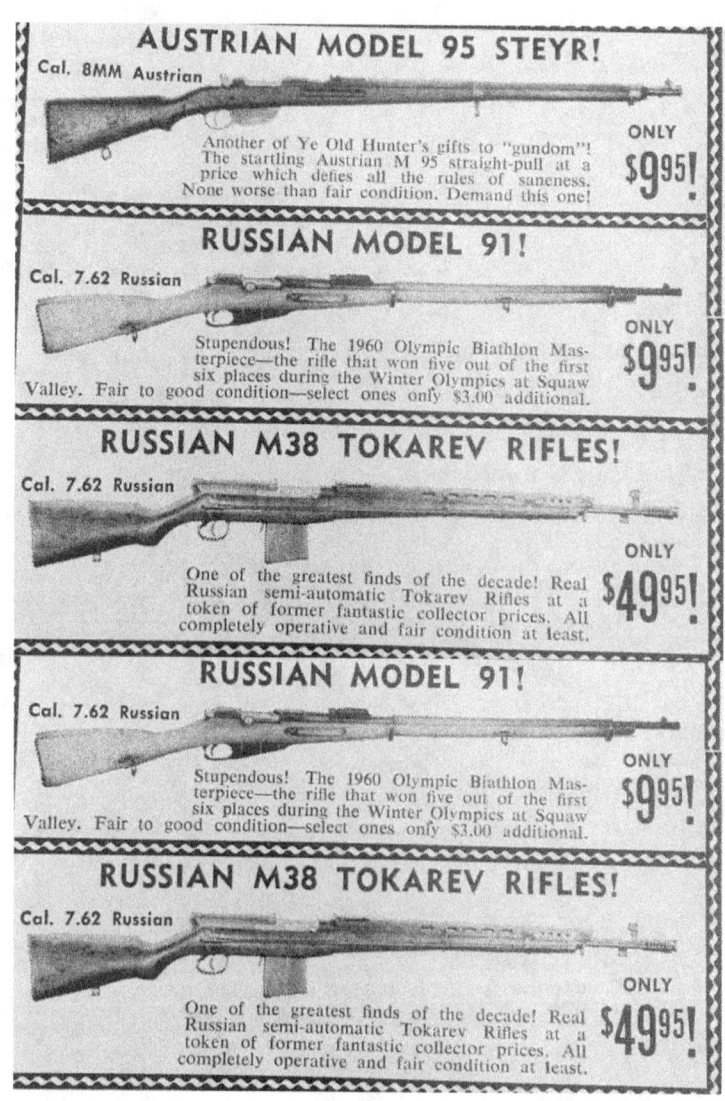

Glossary

Alpha prefix: The letters preceding serial numbers on Soviet and Eastern European Mosin-Nagants represent blocks of 9,999 rifles assigned at random.

Arshin - An archaic Russian unit of measurement used on the M91 rear sights equal to 28 inches or .71 meters.

AZF - Acronym for Artillerie Zeugs Fabrik, an Austrian arsenal mark found on some Mosin Nagant receivers.

Böhler-Stahl - The mark found on the bottom of the barrel shank of Finnish M24 barrels produced in Germany. Bohler is the type of steel, and Stahl is German for steel.

CCCP - Cyrillic initials for Soyuz Sovetskikh Sotsialisticheskikh Republik or Union of Soviet Socialist Republics (USSR).

Chatellerault - The French arms manufacturer that made some of the first Russian M91s.

Civil Guard - A Finnish volunteer organization roughly equivalent to the US National Guard or British Home Guard. See The Suojeluskunta at Mosin Nagant Dot Net for a detailed history.

Continuation War: The war between Finland and the Soviet Union from June 1941 to September 1944 continued the Winter War in which Finland sought to recover lost territory.

Cossack - A short rifle issued to mounted troops sans bayonet and marked Ka3 on the barrel shank. Along with the Dragoon rifle, it was a forerunner of the M91/30.

Counter-bore - Removal of worn rifling at the muzzle by drilling it wider than the bore diameter to improve accuracy.

DDR - Deutsche Demokratische Republik, German Democratic Republic or East Germany.

Dog collar - A small leather strap with a buckle used in pairs to attach a sling to a Mosin Nagant through the sling slots.

Dragoon: The Russian short rifle produced until the early 1930s was the forerunner for the M91/30. It differed from the Cossack in that it was issued and sighted with a bayonet.

Electro penciled - The etching of receivers, bolts, and other parts with a new serial number, often during refurbishment.

Ex-Dragoon - A Dragoon rifle (pre-1930 dated short rifle) updated to M91/30 specifications.

Ex-sniper - A former sniper rifle with its scope mount removed, mounting holes plugged and the bent bolt replaced with a straight one.

Finn matched - A Finnish built or marked rifle with its bolt's serial number renumbered to match the barrel. Even though a buttplate and floorplate numbers may or may not match, it would still be considered Finn matched.

Force matched - A term that describes a rifle with one or more parts renumbered to match the barrel serial number. Telltale signs include a lined out serial number, or the previous number ground off electro-penciled numbers, or numbers lacking an alpha prefix when applicable.

GPW - Great Patriotic War, the Soviet name for World War II.

Hardwood stock - A stock made of solid wood as opposed to laminated wood.

Hex - Early Russian and Soviet receivers have a flat top and angled sides instead of being round.

High wall - A term describing a receiver without the area to the left of the bolt the machined out. Machining facilitated mounting side rail scope mounts as expediency during production from 1941 to 1945.

HV - Häiriövapaa or jamb free. Finnish M28/30 magazines were thus marked to indicate a modification to help prevent rim jams. All M39 magazines have this modification and are not marked.

Instructie - A marking found on Cold War-era Romanian rifles issued to various civil organizations for use in case of an invasion from the West.

Izhevsk - A Russian/Soviet city in the Ural Mountains location of Mosin Nagant production from 1892 to 1948. The arsenal produced the majority of Mosin Nagants during World War II and is now known as Izhmash.

Ka3 - Russian abbreviation for Cossack.

KLP - Kymenlaakson piiri or Kymenlaakson district, found on M24s from the Kymenlaakson Civil Guard district in Finland.

Laminated stock - A rifle stock made of wood sliced in thin layers and glued together for strength and resistance to changes in climate.

Lyogkaya Pulya Stal – *LPS* Light Bullet Steel, spitzer bullet, whose basic design has remained unchanged to the present.

Lotta rifle - Finnish M24s. Called this because they were funded by the Lotta Svärd, or Civil Guard women's auxiliary.

Low wall: A receiver machined down to the left of the bolt. The majority of Mosin production was of this type.

MO - Ministry of Defense (Soviet). See the Mosin Nagant MO Marks page.

NEW - Collectors' abbreviation for New England Westinghouse, which made M91 rifles under contract for Russia during WWI.

NSD - Nylands-Södra distrikt, found on M24s from the **Nylands-Södra** - Civil Guard district in Finland.

OEWG - The abbreviation for Ostereichische Waffenfabrik Gesellschaft, an Austrian arsenal mark found on some Mosin Nagant receivers.

PCFCP - Cyrillic initials for Russian Soviet Federated Socialist Republic (RSFSR).

PE - A Soviet focus adjustable scope produced from 1932 to 1936, an improved version of a Zeiss design.

PEM - A Soviet riflescope produced from 1936 to 1942 that lacked the focus adjustment of the PE.

Peter the Great Russian - the Tsar who founded the Tula arsenal in 1712. Firearms produced at Tula from 1912 were marked Peter the Great until the Bolshevik revolution of 1917.

Popsicle sticks - Reinforcement of the Finnish M27 nose cap to prevent damage to the stock's fore-end when fixing the bayonet.

P Series - M91s that have the barrel relined by the Finns and marked P-26 or P-27 with 26 and 27 representing the year they were relined. Many were not fully assembled until the Winter War.

PU - The final Soviet Mosin Nagant scope design was produced from 1942 to 1944 and intermittently up to 1958. It is smaller than the previous models and is the most commonly encountered in the US.

Puolustuslaitos Defense Department - Finnish mark used for two months in 1942.

Round - The later Soviet receivers without the angular shape of the earlier ones.

SA - Suomen Armeija - Finnish Army property mark used after Puolustuslaitos.

Sako - An abbreviation for Suojeluskuntain Ase-ja Konepaja Oy, a weapons and machine factory of Suojeluskunta (Civil Guard)

SCW - Abbreviation for Spanish Civil War during which Mosins were provided to the Republican side by the Soviet Union.

Sestroryetsk - A northern suburb of St. Petersburg, the location of Mosin Nagant production from 1892 to 1918.

SIG - Schweiz-Industrie Gesellschaft - The Swiss firm that produced M24 and M28 barrels for Finland.

S number - The Civil Guard district number preceded by an S and found on receivers or barrel shanks of Civil Guard rifles.

Stepped barrel: - A heavier barrel found on some Finnish M24s and M91s stepped down near the muzzle to fit a standard M91 bayonet.

Straight barrel - A Finnish M24 barrel that is not heavier and therefore does not have a bayonet step at the muzzle. Much less common than the M24 stepped barrels.

SY - Suojeluskuntain Yliesikunta, the Finnish abbreviation for Civil Guard.

Sk.Y - Suojeluskuntain Yliesikunta - Finnish abbreviation for Civil Guard used after SY.

Three-piece stock - A Finnish stock that is spliced forward of the magazine and at the toe.

Tikkakoski Woodpecker Falls (or Rapids) - A city and firearm manufacturing company located in central Finland, often abbreviated by collectors as Tikka.

Tryokhlineyka - Three-line, an affectionate term for the Mosin-Nagant rifle.

Tula - A Russian/Soviet city south of Moscow, a location of Mosin Nagant production from 1892 to 1944.

Two-piece stock - A Finnish stock spliced forward of the magazine, but not at the toe. A Soviet rifle stock joined at the toe.

V.K.T. - Valtion Kirvääritehdas, Finnish abbreviation for State Firearms Factory. Today known as Valmet.

Winter War - The war between Finland and the Soviet Union from November 1939 to March 1940, a failed attempt by the Soviet Union to gain a buffer zone north of St. Petersburg.

www.ingramcontent.com/pod-product-compliance
Lightning Source LLC
Chambersburg PA
CBHW082244300426
44110CB00036B/2441